Easy Guide to Sewing Blouses

Connie Long

The Taunton Press

Cover Photo: Boyd Hagen

Publisher: Suzanne La Rosa
Acquisitions Editor: Jolynn Gower
Publishing Coordinator: Sarah Coe
Editors: Eileen Hanson, Peter Chapman
Designer: Jodie Delohery
Layout Artist: Lynne Phillips
Illustrator: Clarke Barre
Photographers: Scott Phillips, Boyd Hagen
Typeface: Bookman/Optima
Paper: 70-lb. Warren Patina Matte
Printer: Quebecor Printing Hawkins, New Canton, Tennessee

Taunton
BOOKS & VIDEOS

for fellow enthusiasts

© 1997 by The Taunton Press, Inc.
All rights reserved.

First printing: 1997
Printed in the United States of America

A THREADS Book
THREADS® is a trademark of The Taunton Press, Inc.,
registered in the U.S. Patent and Trademark Office.

The Taunton Press, 63 South Main Street, Box 5506,
Newtown, CT 06470-5506

Library of Congress Cataloging-in-Publication Data

Long, Connie.
        Easy guide to sewing blouses / Connie Long.
            p. cm. — (Sewing companion library)
        "A Threads book" — T.p. verso.
        Includes index.
        ISBN 1-56158-108-9
        1. Blouses. 2. Sewing. I. Title. II. Series.
TT545.L66 1997
646.4'35 — dc20   96-27691
                                             CIP

Introduction

I can still picture the simple blouse I made during my first sewing class. It was a light blue cotton broadcloth with a round neckline and cap sleeves. Although the blouse had many details in common with the pattern I now use to teach beginners how to sew, the construction techniques were quite different. Over the years I've learned a more practical side to sewing and have streamlined my techniques to get wonderful results in considerably less time. My sewing is always evolving to include new methods and new technology while retaining classic methods that still work well.

This book is organized to take you through the blouse-making process from pattern selection to the final details of construction. The pattern, size, and fabric you choose are just as important to the final garment as the construction, and the first two chapters help you make the right choices. Chapter 3 is about fit and pattern adjustment. It is important to define good fit before it can be achieved. An overall smooth appearance and the ability to move in comfort are just two of the things to look for. With all the possible variations in body shape within each size, it is important to learn how to check and adjust the fit. These adjustments change a standard-size pattern into a pattern with a custom fit.

Chapter 4 is about sewing techniques. Use the techniques section to supplement or clarify the pattern directions. For some details, the information is simply more complete than the pattern directions or is presented in a different order. For other details, the directions are a departure from the standard pattern directions. More that one option is often described. The emphasis is on machine sewing, which is consistent with the ready-to-wear look we are striving for.

The information in *Easy Guide to Sewing Blouses* should be useful for sewers of all levels. If you're a beginner or a sewer who hasn't sewn for a while, start with a simple blouse and use a stable fabric such as a cotton broadcloth in a solid color or a small all-over print that doesn't require matching. Then add a new detail or technique with each new project. If you're an intermediate or advanced sewer, select a pattern in the skill level at which you feel comfortable. Look over the guidesheet before buying, and then follow the techniques in this book instead of your pattern. For some details, more than one technique is described— for example, I've included lots of special seams. Try these on your left-over fabric and select the best for each application.

1 Choosing Your Pattern

Pattern shopping is filled with possibilities, and there are lots of wonderful blouse styles to choose from. Before you open a pattern book, evaluate your wardrobe to determine your needs and likes, look at ready-to-wear, and analyze your figure.

Which blouses do you wear the most and always feel good wearing? What is it that you like about each item—its fit, its color? Is it comfortable? Does it complement other garments—and get compliments from others? It's just as important to note the blouses you seldom wear and to understand why. They may be the wrong style or the wrong fit for you, or maybe you just don't have the right thing to go with them.

Get ideas for new and flattering styles by trying on ready-to-wear. Observe fashion trends, paying attention to style lines, necklines, fabric, and flattering details. Use the information in this chapter to determine your best silhouette. Then look at the pattern's silhouette and details. Styles that draw attention around the face and shoulders are flattering to all figure types and are a great choice for business attire.

Commercial blouse patterns are an excellent value. Patterns are available in the latest designer and ready-to-wear styles, and the selection is better than ever. The pattern catalog is organized according to garment type, size, and fashion look. You'll find the newest styles at the beginning of each section. Look for blouses in Separates, Designer, and Sportswear, as well as in the Blouses and Dresses sections. A great blouse pattern may be part of a complete ensemble or the top of a two-piece dress.

Use the information in this chapter to select the best size, too. To select your size, compare your measurements to the standard size chart at the back of the pattern book or on the back of the pattern envelope. For blouses, the critical measurement is the high-bust measurement.

The Best Style for You

The best style is compatible and flattering to your figure, plays up your best features, and draws attention away from your negative ones. Focus on the basic silhouette first, and then look at the details.

Analyzing Your Figure

Analyze your body shape and proportions to help you select styles that conform to your body's natural silhouette or balance your figure. Basic body shape is defined by the relationship between the width of the shoulders, waist, and hips. The outline connecting these points forms one of four shapes: H (rectangular), X (hourglass), A (pear), or Y (wedge). To determine your body silhouette, position a straightedge at the side of your torso connecting the fullest part of the hips to the shoulders.

Natural and Optional Silhouettes

■ **Rectangular**   ✕ **Hourglass**

■ Most harmonious silhouette	✕ Most harmonious silhouette
✕ Create the illusion of a narrower waist with seams or a loose belt.	■ Select straight seams and bypass the waist.
▲ Narrow the shoulders with raglan sleeves or halter necklines.	▲ Narrow the shoulders with raglan seams or halter necklines.
▼ Widen or accent the shoulders, keep the body narrow.	▼ Extend or focus on the shoulders.

H or rectangular: Shoulders are as wide as hips. The straightedge is perpendicular to the floor with little or no waist indentation.

X or hourglass: Shoulders are as wide as hips, with a nipped-in waist. The straightedge is perpendicular to the floor, and there is a definite indentation at the waist.

A or pear: Shoulders and waist are narrower than hips. The straightedge is farther out at the hips.

Y or wedge: Shoulders are wider than waist and hips. The straightedge is farther out at the shoulders.

Clothing with the same silhouette as the body is the easiest to wear and requires the fewest adjustments. You can wear other silhouettes to add variety to your wardrobe or to balance your figure (remember, the blouse and skirt or pants complete the total silhouette). For example, to change an H body to a Y silhouette, select an extended-shoulder style that is narrow at the hem. To change an H body to an A silhouette, create the illusion of narrow shoulders with raglan sleeves or a halter neckline and flare the hem.

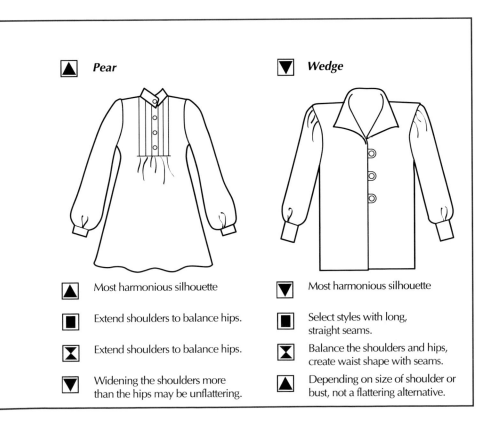

▲ *Pear*

▲ Most harmonious silhouette

■ Extend shoulders to balance hips.

⧖ Extend shoulders to balance hips.

▼ Widening the shoulders more than the hips may be unflattering.

▼ *Wedge*

▼ Most harmonious silhouette

■ Select styles with long, straight seams.

⧖ Balance the shoulders and hips, create waist shape with seams.

▲ Depending on size of shoulder or bust, not a flattering alternative.

Choosing the Best Style for Your Figure

The inside lines of a garment influence the total design.

Horizontal vs. Vertical

The eye reads horizontal lines first. Place them in flattering places—for example, a horizontal yoke seam on an extended shoulder to balance wide hips.

One vertical line is good, but two or more can sometimes be better. Vertical lines lead the eye up and down and have a slimming effect, but repetition and placement make a difference. When placed far apart or repeated at even intervals, vertical lines draw the eye across the figure and it appears wider and shorter.

Diagonals

Diagonals lengthen or shorten the figure depending on how long they are, and at what angle.

Curved Lines

Curved lines produce the same effect as straight lines when placed in the same position. The curved seam is more graceful and conforms well to body contours.

The Best Pattern for You

To choose a blouse pattern, take a closer look at the pattern details. Some of the details affect the shape of the silhouette, while others are functional or add design interest.

Select design elements that are flattering to your size and shape and project the image you want. You'll find many variations of different looks (fashionable, classic, etc.) in the pattern catalog. The photos in the catalog bring a garment to life and project a desired image. Use the drawings that accompany the photos to see details and seamlines more clearly.

Use the pattern envelope, as well as the pattern guidesheet, to evaluate and compare patterns. Check the widths and lengths chart. These measurements give you a clear point of comparison when the details look the same. You may find that styles that look similar are inches apart in width or length.

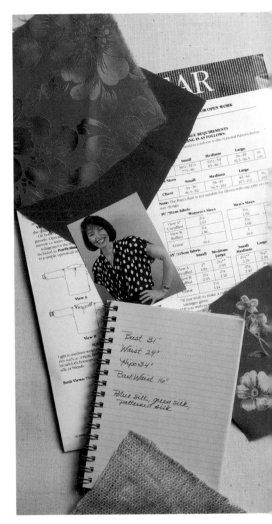

Reading the Pattern Envelope

Back views of the pattern show the construction details. When space allows, front views are also provided.

The **garment description** starts with the garment category (such as "Misses' blouse") and includes details that may not be visible from the photo or drawings, such as hidden closures or pockets. Other pertinent information, such as "no provision for above-waist adjustment" and "purchased belt," appears here. Fitting terms, such as "loose fitting," are included to help you understand the amount of ease allowed. Look at the ease chart at the back of the pattern book to understand how much ease to expect (for more on ease, see the sidebar on p. 30).

Notions are listed separately for each view. These include buttons, shoulder pads, elastic, zippers, and snaps (but not lining,

Choose patterns according to your skill level. Before buying a pattern, look over the guidesheet and see if you can follow the directions. Keep in mind that a simple cap-sleeve blouse pattern labeled "easy to sew" is not the same as a button-front blouse pattern with a yoke, collar, and cuffs also labeled "easy to sew." Both are easy compared to another garment with similar details, but not when compared to each other.

The *width at lower edge* is especially useful in selecting a pattern. It tells you at a glance how much fullness is in the garment. For example, if the hip measurement for a size 12 is 36 in. and the width at lower edge for the blouse you are sewing is 40 in., then the amount of ease at the lower edge is exactly 4 in.

interfacing, and thread). Sizes and quantity are also included, such as "eight ⅝-in. buttons" or "½-in. covered shoulder pads."

Fabrics listed are those that the designer considers best suited for the style. "Crisp" or "soft" fabrics are often indicated. This section also lets you know when the style is not suitable for "obvious diagonals," plaids, stripes, or napped fabrics. If the pattern is suitable for these, the statement "allow extra fabric to match plaids or stripes" lets you know.

The abbreviation "w/wo nap" refers to how the pattern pieces are laid out on the fabric. "With-nap" layouts have the top of all the pattern pieces placed in the same direction (toward the same cut edge or cross grain). Layouts for fabrics without nap may have the tops of the pattern pieces facing in either direction (toward either cut edge or cross grain). Nap not only refers to napped or pile fabrics such as velvet or corduroy, but also to other fabrics that show shading, such as satin and knits. Nap also refers to a directional print, such as a rose print where all the stems are going in the same direction. Take a good look at your print; sometimes a print that appears to be without a nap has one repeat that follows a single direction.

The **yardage chart** has the sizes printed across the top. Each garment style or view is listed vertically. The amount of fabric you need depends on your size, the view you are sewing, and the width of your fabric.

Finished garment measurements tell you the finished back length of the garment from the prominent bone at the back of the neck to the finished hemline. This measurement gives you a pretty accurate idea of the length, even on scooped or low-neckline styles. Also given is the finished width at the lower edge of the garment, and sometimes the width in the hip or bust area.

Which Size to Buy?

When choosing a blouse pattern, forget the size you buy in ready-to-wear. Standard body measurements for pattern sizes are completely different from those used by clothing companies. Select the pattern size according to your body measurements. For blouses, jackets, dresses, and any other garments that include the upper body, the critical measurement is the high-bust or chest measurement. Measure the chest circumference just under the arms (see the drawing on p. 26). If you take your own measurement, be sure to lower your elbows to your sides before reading the tape (having your elbows raised can affect the measurement). Compare your high-bust measurement to the full-bust measurement on the pattern to select the size.

If you fall between two sizes, you may go a size larger or smaller. The amount of ease in the style can help you decide which is better. For example, if the blouse is oversized and you are petite but busty, select the smaller size. If the blouse is close-fitting and you have broad shoulders, select the larger size. Even if your hips are two or three sizes larger than your bust, you should still select the pattern according to your high-bust measurement. Hip adjustments are easy to make.

Multisized patterns   Many patterns are multisized, with three or more sizes per pattern. Multisized patterns are convenient to use and adjust since so many of us have multisized bodies. The cutting lines, notches, and dots are printed with different types of lines to differentiate between the different sizes. For example, the largest size in the size group is usually printed with a solid line. Other sizes have dotted lines or dashes so you can tell them apart. Be extra careful where the lines cross over each other at necklines and armholes. Because of the way patterns are graded, the cutting line for the largest size doesn't always stay outermost. Highlight your cutting line in these areas to avoid mistakes.

CHOOSING A PATTERN WITH A FABRIC IN MIND

Solids
Show off great style line and topstitching (but also sewing mistakes); most flexible choice.

Prints
Seams (and minor sewing flaws) don't show; for large repeats and plaids, select patterns with fewer seams.

Silky fabrics
Conform to the figure shape; select loose-fitting patterns with soft details, no darts; pleats or gathers work well; fewer seams are better; oversized and voluminous styles look good and create a fluid silhouette that is flattering to most figures.

Crisp fabrics
Show off the style's silhouette; better for styles with controlled fullness; darts and style seams advisable; not good for yokes with gathers for most people (add too much volume).

Sheers
Seams become part of the design, so the fewer seams the better; consider a pattern without facings or replace them with bindings if they work for the shape of the neckline (for example, bindings work for a scooped neckline but not for a sweetheart neckline). Having facings may be fine—imagine seeing them through the blouse; is it a pleasing line or too busy? If it's too busy, choose a simpler pattern.

2 Selecting Fabrics and Notions

For me, the fabric is the most important ingredient in a blouse. A beautiful fabric doesn't need a special pattern, and it can make a simple pattern special. Very often I buy the fabric long before committing to a specific style. Like other fabric lovers, the fabric finds me while I casually browse and enjoy the colors and textures around me. That special fabric attracts my attention because it's the perfect complement to so many things in my wardrobe...and because I love the color.

Use this chapter to help select the perfect fabric for your blouse. Consider your fashion image (e.g., tailored, sophisticated, dramatic, romantic, casual), your lifestyle, and your skill level. Some fabrics like silk charmeuse and silk chiffon require greater skill. Others like linen are a pleasure to sew but require lots of pressing.

Decide what fabric qualities are most important to you (such as durability, comfort, wrinkle resistance) and select the most suitable fabric. Choose a fabric that's flattering and appropriate for the pattern and how often it will be worn—an evening blouse doesn't need to be durable, but a wardrobe basic does. The back of the pattern envelope lists recommended fabrics, but keep in mind that other fabrics with a similar weight and drape are also suitable.

The right decisions about interfacings and notions contribute to the overall quality of the blouse. The interfacing, needle size, and thread type and size must be compatible with the fashion fabric. When interfacing is indicated on the pattern, I like to use fusible interfacing because it's easier to handle and gives the best results.

Shoulder pads come in a variety of shapes and thicknesses. The best ones to use are proportioned to the blouse silhouette, the sleeve shape, and the wearer. Select buttons that blend in or enliven the style to add the finishing touch to your blouse.

Fashion Fabric Options

Selecting fabric is a visual and tactile experience. Drape the fabric on yourself in front of a mirror to get the whole picture. Look for the recommended fabrics as well as other fabrics with the same weight and drape. Also consider the fabric's durability and maintenance. Some fabrics are more time-consuming to sew and require greater sewing skills. Learn which fabrics are easier to sew and how to identify a quality fabric.

A single fabric may not have all the properties you would like in a fabric. Decide what is most important to the style and your skill level. Fabrics are available in different fibers. Charmeuse and crêpe de chine may be silk or polyester; broadcloth may be cotton, silk, rayon, or a blend of fibers.

When choosing a blouse fabric, you need to consider the fiber content, the weight and drape, and the design of the fabric to achieve the best results for the blouse style, your needs, and your skill level.

Fiber (natural, synthetics, or blends): Natural fibers with a stable weave (such as cotton broadcloth, dotted Swiss, lawn, and sateen) are easier to cut and sew than synthetics. Seams press beautifully and look well made. Natural fibers are moisture-absorbent and more comfortable to wear. Synthetics require less maintenance (such as ironing) and generally wrinkle less after sewing. They are non-moisture-absorbent and can feel clammy in warm temperatures. Blends combine the low maintenance of synthetics with the comfort of natural fibers.

Weight and drape: Crisp fabrics (such as cotton or silk poplin, cotton piqué, Thai silk, and silk organza) are easier to cut and sew and are good for styles with controlled shape. They emphasize the style's silhouette. Soft fabrics (such as silk or polyester, crêpe de chine, charmeuse, and wool challis) conform to the body; they can have more fullness in the silhouette. These fabrics are more time-consuming to cut and sew and require greater skill.

Design: Solid fabrics show the style lines of the garment, whereas prints obscure them. Prints that don't need matching are a good choice for beginners because minor stitching imperfections are also hidden. Styles with lots of seams are inappropriate for large prints and large plaids and require extra time for matching.

Silky fabrics are not for beginners. Choose a very simple pattern as your first sewing project in a silky. A pure-silk silky is easier to sew with professional results than a polyester silky.

Use the envelope suggestions as a general guide to select the best fabric for your blouse. Sometimes a "crisp" or "soft" fabric is specified in order to achieve the silhouette or construction techniques successfully. Examples are collars or ruffles that are meant to stand up crisply or gathers and draped neckline treatments that are intended to be soft.

WHAT TO LOOK FOR IN A FABRIC

• Check for wrinkle recovery. All natural fibers wrinkle to some degree, especially linen. How quickly fabrics shed wrinkles is affected by many things, including the quality, length, and type of fiber, and the density and type of weave. Use the "crush test" to determine how the fabric performs. Crush the fabric in the palm of your hand for a few seconds and release. The fabric that springs back will resist wrinkles. If wrinkles remain, you can expect the same from your garment.

• Check that the cross threads (weft yarns) meet the selvages at right angles. This shows that the fabric is on grain. Permanent-press fabrics that are not on grain are impossible to straighten.

• Never buy a fabric with a *printed* check, plaid, or horizontal stripes. These patterns are impossible to print on grain, forcing you to decide whether to cut the garment on grain or so that the pattern looks straight—a no-win situation.

Woven versions are always on grain. A woven pattern looks almost the same on both sides. You can identify a print by looking at the wrong side of the fabric, which will be much lighter.

• A firm weave with a high thread count is more durable and holds its shape better.

• The weave and color should be even. Always check the fold for fading.

How Much Fabric to Buy

The pattern's yardage requirement (including with-nap yardage for directional fabrics) is tested and accurate. However, there are situations when you need to buy more fabric than specified:

• When using washable fabrics that shrink (most natural fibers).

• For matching prints or plaids with large repeats (the length of the repeat can be anywhere from 1 in. to over ¾ yd.). Allow one extra repeat per garment length; for example, if it takes two blouse lengths and one sleeve length of fabric, buy three extra repeats for maximum flexibility.

• When you lengthen (or sometimes widen) the pattern and bring it into another size range.

• To allow for straightening the cross grain (this is not necessary if the yardage is torn by the salesperson instead of cut).

• When the fabric measures less than the specified width (45 in. or 60 in.). You can get a clue as to whether you need to buy more fabric by looking at the cutting layout. If the same cutting layout is used for several sizes and your size is one of the smaller sizes, you probably don't need to buy more fabric. If your size is the largest size in the layout, you do. The conversion chart at the back of the pattern book is also helpful in these situations; it gives you the equal number of square inches, though they may not be in the configuration you need.

PREPARING FABRIC FOR SEWING

If you plan to wash the blouse, the general rule is to prewash the fabric using the same method. I prefer not to use soap, just water, and then dry using the permanent-press cycle to continue the shrinking process. Always test-wash a swatch first. Look for bleeding or fading color. White vinegar will help set the color if there is minor bleeding. (Use ¼ to ½ cup of white vinegar to a gallon of cool water; soak for 10 minutes, gently moving the fabric, and then rinse with cool water.) Also look for undesirable changes in the texture of the fabric. A transparent, gauzy fabric may shrink and become heavy and almost opaque.

I usually dry-clean dark or brightly colored fabrics even if they are a washable cotton to keep the color like new, but I'll hand-wash most silks, especially if the color is white or pale. Many silks, such as crêpe de chine, charmeuse, and broadcloth, wash beautifully (wash them with shampoo to help them keep their lustrous finish). Expect more shrinkage and a greater textural change from silk georgette and chiffon; I often end up dry-cleaning these. Raw silks don't usually wash well, but it's worth testing any silk.

Another consideration is how complicated the style is to press: If the style requires a lot of pressing, you can prewash the fabric but dry-clean the garment. Prewashing the fabric gives you the option of washing when the garment gets older or if you're traveling and dry cleaning is not an option.

Interfacings and Notions

Choose interfacing according to the fabric weight and type of shaping required, such as firm or soft shaping. The interfacing should not overpower the fashion fabric and must be compatible with its care requirements. Basic notions such as needles and thread must also be compatible with the fashion fabric.

Interfacings

Interfacing is the inner layer used in areas of the blouse that need extra support, such as necklines, facings, collars, cuffs, and buttonholes. Its purpose is to support the shape, maintain the crispness, or add stability to areas that get stressed.

If you make the right choice, fusible interfacings are easier and faster to use than sew-in interfacings and result in professional-looking blouses. The key to making the right choice is to know what types are available and what kind of support they provide.

Choosing an Interfacing   There are three basic types of fusible interfacings: woven, nonwoven, and knit. The one you choose will depend on how much stability or control the fashion fabric and style require.

Woven interfacings have a lengthwise and crosswise grain just like woven fabrics, giving them lengthwise and crosswise stability. Cut wovens on the straight of grain for control or on the bias for softer support.

Nonwoven interfacings, which are the easiest to use for beginners, are made of bonded synthetic fibers. A wide range of support is available, including stable, crosswise stretch, and all-bias. Stable has crisp shaping; it has no stretch and can be cut in any direction. Crosswise stretch is a stable interfacing combining crosswise stretch and lengthwise stability. For best results, keep the pattern grainline parallel to the stable lengthwise edge. All-bias has stretch in all directions and provides the softest shaping.

Cool-fuse interfacings provide soft shaping for lightweight fabrics.

Most interfacings are preshrunk—check the label. If fusible interfacings are not preshrunk, soak them in warm water for 15 minutes. Do not wring. Blot excess water and line-dry or drip-dry over a basin. Remove wrinkles from improper storage by rewetting and drip-drying.

Knit interfacings, which offer the most natural and flexible support, are available in three basic types: tricot, weft insertion, and warp insertion. Tricot-knit interfacings have lengthwise stability and crosswise stretch; use them for soft and supple shaping. Weft-insertion interfacings have a stable crosswise and lengthwise direction; use them when you want stable support that is more supple than a woven interfacing. Warp-insertion interfacings have stretch in all directions; use them for the softest shaping and drapability.

The only drawback to using a fusible interfacing is that you really can't determine the hand until after you fuse the interfacing to the fashion fabric. To evaluate the hand and drape, test-fuse interfacing to a small piece of fabric. The fabric surface should be smooth and unchanged. Check for show-through on whites and pastel shades. Fabrics with texture or embossing can be fused on the undercollar instead of the top collar, or you may need to use a sew-in interfacing.

You see blouses without interfacing both in inexpensive ready-to-wear and expensive designer lines. If you opt to do without the interfacing, meticulous sewing is a must; otherwise, you'll end up with stretched necklines and puckered buttonholes.

INTERFACINGS FOR SILKY FABRICS

Lightweight silky fabrics and fabrics that must be pressed with cooler temperatures require special interfacings. Cool-fuse interfacings, which bond when pressed with the iron temperature set at a silk, are perfect for heat-sensitive fibers like synthetics and silks. Other fusible interfacings may cause spots on silky fabrics as the fusing agents penetrate to the surface of the fabric. Cool-fuse choices include:

SofTouch
Nonwoven brushed surface; 100% nylon, washable, and dry-cleanable; soft shaping

SofBrush
Warp-insertion brushed knit, all-bias; 100% polyester, washable, and dry-cleanable; soft tailoring, supple shaping

SofKnit
Diamond-pattern knit fabric, all-bias; 100% nylon; softest shaping and most drapable

So Sheer
Semi-sheer tricot-knit fabric, stable in lengthwise direction, stretch in crosswise direction; excellent for most sheer fabrics

If you like the hand of these cool-fuse interfacings, you can also use them with fabrics other than silk. I use SofTouch and SofBrush on linen, cotton, and wool challis for the softest shaping.

Notions for Sewing

Notions play an important supporting role in creating a beautiful blouse. Use this section to help select the right thread, needle, shoulder pads, and buttons.

Thread   Selecting the right thread means more than just choosing the right color. All-purpose threads can be used on a variety of fabrics for both machine and hand sewing. Choose a thread that's compatible with the fabric weight and fiber. I prefer to use 100% polyester thread because it is strong, elastic, and doesn't shrink in the dryer. I use it on all types of fabrics unless the perfect color is not available or I need to go to a finer thread.

100% cotton thread is suitable for natural fibers. Because it does not have enough stretch, it is not suitable for knits and woven garments with bias-cut seams.

100% polyester thread is suitable for synthetic and natural fibers as well as for all types of knits.

Cotton-covered polyester thread is suitable for all fabric types.

Extra-fine cotton-covered polyester thread is good for lightweight fabrics.

Fine cotton machine-embroidery thread can be used for double-sewn seams on extra-fine fabrics. This is a two-ply thread (all-purpose threads are three-ply).

Size A silk thread produces beautiful buttonholes on fine silks. This thread is also nice to use for buttonholes in natural fibers.

The thread color appears lighter after sewing. For the best match, select a color a shade darker than the fashion fabric. For tweeds, plaids, or prints, the best match may be the background color or a greyed version of one of the colors.

Needles   Needle size must be compatible with the fashion fabric and the thread being used. For sewing blouse-weight fabrics, use universal needles size 9, 10, or 11. Replace a used needle with a new one of the appropriate size for new projects on fine fabrics.

Extra-fine sheers and tightly woven fabrics such as satin, taffeta, silk broadcloth, and China silk may require needles with a sharp point rather than with a universal point. Use a jeans needle size 10/70 or Microtex size 10/70, 8/60, or 6/50 on these fabrics. Extra-fine sizes 8/60 and 6/50 must be used with extra-fine two-ply thread, such as fine machine-embroidery thread.

Always test your needle on the fabric. The main reason for pulls in the fabric is that the needle is too large (another reason is that the thread is too thick or strong).

Shoulder Pads   Shoulder silhouettes change with fashion trends, creating the need for a variety of shoulder-pad shapes that support these varied shoulder lines. Styles with exaggerated shoulders need the most support, but even natural-shoulder fashions benefit from thin shoulder support for smooth and

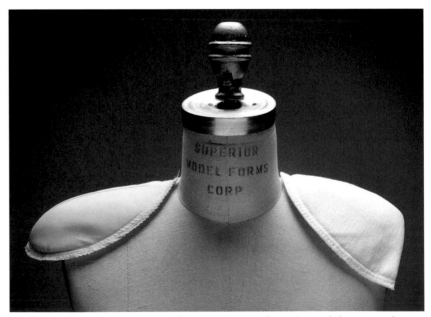

Raglan and set-in shoulder pads come in a wide variety of shapes and thicknesses. Shown here are two raglan pads with very different shapes.

subtle shaping. If you have narrow or sloping shoulders use shoulder pads to balance your silhouette.

There are two basic types of shoulder pads: set-in pads and raglan pads. Set-in shoulder pads have a triangular shape and a wedge profile that is thick at the armhole edge and thin at the neck edge. Thickness can range from ¼ in. to 1 in. Set-in pads, not surprisingly, are appropriate for set-in sleeves. Some set-in pads are designed for set-in sleeves that extend beyond the natural shoulder line.

Raglan pads curve over the shoulders. These pads are shaped to blend the shoulder curve into the sleeve and avoid a ridge on the outer garment. Thicknesses range from ¼ in. to 1 in. Raglan pads are perfect for dolman, raglan, and kimono sleeves. They are also appropriate for most dropped-shoulder set-in sleeves.

The commercial pattern lists the type and thickness of pad required to duplicate the fit. The pattern is drafted for a particular-size shoulder pad, and this amount is added to the armhole and sleeve. However, individual shoulder lines vary—a person with sloping shoulders may need to use a thicker pad to keep the same shoulder line, while a person with square shoulders will require less padding. The other option is to adjust the shoulder line. Uneven shoulders will require extra padding on one side so that they appear to be even.

Buttons   More than any other closure, buttons can be functional and decorative at the same time. The notions section of the pattern envelope lists how many and what size buttons to buy. You can vary from that size up to ¼ in. larger or smaller without having to change the amount of overlap on the blouse.

For best results when selecting the buttons, bring along the fabric or a swatch. Buttons must be compatible with the fashion fabric—for example, use lightweight buttons on lightweight fabrics so as not to distort the closure. Be sure the buttons can be cared for the same way as the blouse fabric.

The two basic button types are shank and sew-through. On a shank button, the shank raises the button above the fabric and the thread does not show on top. Shank buttons work nicely with fabric and thread loops as well as buttonholes. Sew-through buttons have two or four holes and are usually flat. Sew these flat to the surface of the fabric only for decorative purposes. Otherwise, they require a thread shank to raise them above the garment. This way, the fabric fits smoothly when buttoned.

Buttons can be decorative as well as functional. Choose them carefully for the perfect finishing touch to your blouse.

3 | *Fitting Your Pattern*

You don't have to be an expert pattern maker to sew custom-made clothes. The key to good fit is to take accurate measurements and then compare them to the pattern standards. Choosing the right size eliminates unnecessary adjustments. Use this chapter to learn how your figure varies from the pattern standard and how to go about making changes to the pattern.

Adjustments turn a standard size into a custom fit. The goal is to present the figure as well balanced, well proportioned, and as attractive as possible. Make all obvious adjustments to the pattern before you cut the fashion fabric, and then check the fit as you sew. As you sew more blouses, your personal pattern adjustments become easier and predictable, and of course faster to accomplish.

Some pattern changes have nothing to do with figure variations. Make changes to allow for turn-of-cloth and to refine the fit of collars and cuffs. Simplify the pattern if you're working with a fabric that is difficult to sew or a print that is busy or difficult to match. Change a patch pocket to a welt pocket. Add a hidden closure to any blouse for a sleek look.

Whether you use a rotary cutter or scissors, accurate cutting lays the foundation for a beautiful blouse. A well-cut edge is the best reference point for sewing a straight seam. Notches and match points facilitate joining blouse pieces with different shapes and controlling ease. Marks also prevent you from making mistakes, as long as you don't ignore the signs.

Comparing Measurements

Fitting the pattern changes the pattern standards to fit and flatter your figure variations. First, you need to determine what those variations are by taking accurate measurements and pin-fitting the pattern.

Measuring Your Body

You'll need some help to take some of the measurements. Wear undergarments or a leotard and measure close to the skin without binding. To find your waist measurement, tie a length of narrow elastic around it and bend from side to side. Leave the elastic on to measure the back-waist length—from the prominent bone at the back of the neck to the waist. If you have trouble determining which bone to use, wear a necklace and measure from the necklace to the bottom of the elastic.

Measure the shoulder width from the neck to the arm. The necklace at the neck makes it easier to determine where the shoulder begins, especially if you have sloping shoulders. To determine the end of the shoulder, raise your arm. The bend at the socket is where the shoulder ends and the arm begins. Measure the sleeve length from the prominent bone at the shoulder to the prominent bone at the wrist. For extended-shoulder, raglan, or dolman sleeve styles, use the combined neck-to-wrist measurement.

Use the bottom chart on the facing page to record your measurements, adding "ease" where necessary to allow for normal body movement. (Ease is the difference between the size measurement on the pattern envelope and the actual measurement of the pattern.) As the size gets larger, the amount of ease required increases as well. The minimum ease requirement is indicated on the chart where it applies. If no amount is indicated, there's no need to allow any ease.

Measuring Your Body

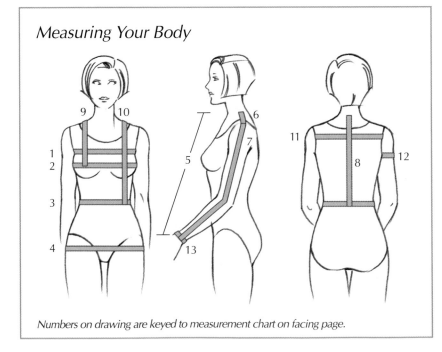

Numbers on drawing are keyed to measurement chart on facing page.

Use the high-bust measurement to select the pattern size. Use the full-bust and full-hip measurements to adjust the pattern width. You need the waist measurement and back-waist length only if the blouse or bodice has waist definition. Otherwise, check the finished blouse length to see if you need to make length adjustments. To adjust the sleeve length, use either the neck-to-wrist or the sleeve-length measurement, depending on the type of sleeve you are sewing.

You won't need to compare all these measurements every time you sew, just the ones that relate to the project you are working on and to your figure variations. Patterns are made to fit an average B-cup figure, so technically any size greater needs a full-bust

SIZING CHART (in inches)

Size	6	8	10	12	14	16	18	20
Bust	30½	31½	32½	34	36	38	40	42
Waist	23	24	25	26½	28	30	32	34
Hips	32½	33½	34½	36	38	40	42	44

MEASUREMENT CHART (in inches)

	Body +	Minimum Ease	= Total
1 High bust (directly under arms)			
2 Bust (fullest level)		2 to 4	
3 Waist		½ to 1½	
4 Hips (at fullest level; note distance to waist)		2 to 3	
5 Neck to wrist (arm bent)			
6 Shoulder (width)			
7 Sleeve length (shoulder to wrist; arm bent)			
8 Back waist (length; if waist is defined)			
9 Shoulder seam to bust point			
10 Front waist (length from shoulder)			
11 Upper back (width 4 in. down from neck)		½ to 1	
12 Upper arm (circumference)		2	
13 Wrist (circumference)		½ to 1½	

adjustment. The style's silhouette and your posture and size play into this adjustment as well; it's possible to be a small size and wear a D cup and not need the adjustment. Here's the checkpoint: When the back length is correct the front-waist length should also be correct. If the front-waist length is too short, use the full-bust adjustment. (If the difference is ½ in. or less and the blouse is worn tucked in, I wouldn't make the adjustment.) This adjustment increases the width and length of the front to accommodate a full or prominent bust. The difference in the length helps you determine how much to lengthen the front.

PIN-FITTING THE PATTERN

Pin-fitting the pattern is another way to determine which adjustments you need to make to the pattern. Pin-fit the pattern tissue to get the overall look and proportion of the blouse. Trim the pattern close to the cutting line at the neck seam and armscye, but leave wide margins at the side seams and shoulders. Press the pattern tissue with a dry iron.

Overlap the seams, or turn one seam under to pin. Don't attach the sleeves. Carefully try on the pattern and pin the center front and back to your clothing; alternatively, you can tie a narrow elastic band around your chest and hips and pin the pattern to the elastic.

Check the following:

• Shoulder width and slope; also check the angle—does it follow the center of your shoulder?

• Dart and pocket placement

• Position of bust point

• Front width—for a large bust, does the bust pull the blouse toward the front or lift the front hem? Also check the back width.

• Side seams—do they hang straight?

Pin-fit the pattern to check the shoulder width and slope.

Adjusting the Pattern

Make general length and width adjustments first, and then work on specific figure variations.

Adjusting the Length

Begin with the length adjustments. Consider the back-waist length only if the style has shaping at the sides, back, or waist. Otherwise, just consider the total garment length. Also make adjustments to the sleeve length as necessary.

Overall Length On a blouse with straight side seams, lengthen or shorten the pattern at the adjustment line or at the bottom. Blouses with slits, curved hems, or other details at the lower edge must be adjusted at the adjustment line.

Back-Waist Length Adjust the pattern front and back between the adjustment lines. To shorten, pleat out the desired amount. To lengthen, cut the pattern between the adjustment lines, separate the pattern, and add an insert. On blank paper, use a clear ruler to draw two parallel lines the desired distance apart. Cut inserts, leaving margins on both sides. Insert the lines between the cut edges. Be sure to line up the center-front or center-back fold and grainline before taping in

place. Blend the cutting lines at the sides of the pattern.

Sleeve Length The measurement you use to adjust the sleeve length depends on the type of sleeve you are sewing.

Standard set-in sleeve: Measure the pattern length, excluding the seam and hem allowance. Compare to your sleeve-length measurement, and lengthen or shorten at the adjustment line. If there are two adjustment lines, divide the amount in two and adjust at both lines.

Raglan sleeve, kimono sleeve: Measure the pattern sleeve length and compare to your neck-to-wrist measurement. If there's a difference, adjust the sleeve length at the adjustment line.

Extended shoulder, dropped shoulder: Measure and add together the pattern shoulder width and the sleeve length. This measurement (excluding the seam and hem allowance) must equal your neck-to-wrist measurement. If there is also a cuff, the shoulder width plus sleeve length plus finished cuff length must equal your neck-to-wrist measurement. If there's any difference, adjust the sleeve length.

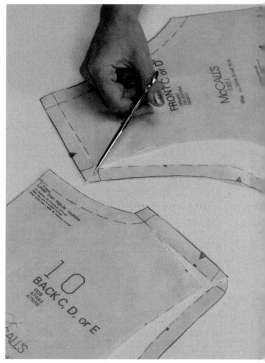

Patterns can be adjusted by spreading or overlapping seam allowances.

For accurate shoulder-width measurement on a yoked blouse, don't use the front edge. Draw in and measure the shoulder placement on the yoke pattern.

Adjusting the Width

When you choose your size by matching your high-bust measurement to the pattern's full-bust measurement (see pp. 12-13), you need to adjust the pattern if your full-bust and hip measurements put you in a different size.

Bust and Hip Width To change the blouse width, compare your full-bust and full-hip measurements to the standard measurements for the size you are using (see the sizing chart on p. 27). Determine the difference for each area and divide by 4. Add or subtract one-quarter the difference to each side seam. Add tissue to the pattern if there is not enough room for adjustment. As an example, to add 1 in. to the bust add $1/4$ in. at each side seam. To add 2 in. to the hips add $1/2$ in. to each side seam and blend the lines.

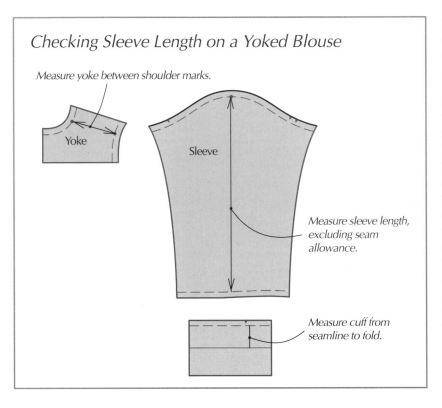

Checking Sleeve Length on a Yoked Blouse

Measure yoke between shoulder marks.

Yoke

Sleeve

Measure sleeve length, excluding seam allowance.

Measure cuff from seamline to fold.

UNDERSTANDING EASE

The difference between the width of your garment and the size of your body is called *ease.* A minimum amount of ease is necessary for comfort and movement. Any extra ease is called *design ease,* which can be anything the designer wants it to be.

Compare your bust and hip measurements to the sizing chart (see p. 27) and note the differences. One way to adjust the width is to increase or decrease the pattern by this amount. For example, if the pattern fits a 34-in. bust and your bust measures 35 in., increase the total bust width by 1 in. This way you maintain the same amount of ease the designer had in mind. This method works well for very close-fitting bodices and for blouses with shoulder pleats.

Another way to make width adjustments is to compare your bust and hip measurements to the finished-garment measurements. Many pattern companies print the finished bust and hip measurements right on the pattern tissue. If your pattern does not provide these measurements, flat-measure the pattern at the bust and hip; don't include seam allowances, darts, or areas that overlap. The finished-garment measurement minus your bust or hip measurement equals the amount of ease. An oversized pattern may eliminate the need for any width adjustments.

Full Bust and Back Width

In addition to the overall width adjustment, you can also make just the front bigger to allow for a full bust. Use the seam method to make this adjustment, separating the seam allowance from the rest of the pattern only in the area that needs adjusting. (The seam method works especially well for making changes that affect two or more adjacent seams, such as the back-width, full-bust, or shoulder and armscye adjustment.)

Starting at the bottom, cut the side seam along the sewing line on the blouse front. When you get to the armscye, continue cutting along the armscye sewing line until you reach the shoulder seam. Clip diagonally to the corner without cutting through the edge at the shoulder and underarm seams. The diagonal clips form hinges that facilitate spreading or overlapping the pattern.

Spread the pattern out and down. If necessary, tuck the armscye along the outer edge to help it lie flat. Spread the width approximately $1/2$ in. for a size C, $3/4$ in. for a D, and $1 1/8$ in. for a DD. Place some pattern tissue under the gap and tape the seams in position (see the drawing at right). Lengthen approximately the same amount at the center front and curve into the original length at the side seam. You can also determine how much length to add by using measurements 8 and 10 on the chart on p. 27.

To make the adjustment for a full back, use the same principle as for a full bust but don't add to the length. On the back pattern piece,

WORKING WITH MULTISIZED PATTERNS

Multisized patterns with three sizes list three sets of measurements. A nice thing about multisized patterns is that you can easily use one size for the shoulders, neck, and armholes, another size for the full bust, and a third size for the hips. For example, if your high-bust measurement puts you in a size 8, your full-bust measurement puts you in a size 10, and your hip measurement puts you in a size 12, blend the three sizes to conform to your shape. Cut out the neck, shoulders, and armhole in a size 8. Go out to a size 10 at the underarm, and blend to a size 12 at the hips. Cut the sleeve width in a size 10 and the sleeve cap in a size 8 to match the armhole.

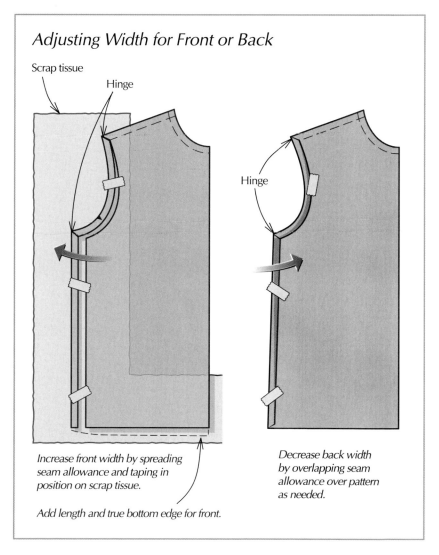

Adjusting Width for Front or Back

Scrap tissue

Hinge

Hinge

Increase front width by spreading seam allowance and taping in position on scrap tissue.

Add length and true bottom edge for front.

Decrease back width by overlapping seam allowance over pattern as needed.

start on the side-seam sewing line near the bottom. Don't cut through the bottom edge but clip diagonally to the corner, forming a hinge. (If you also have a full derriere, clip all the way through the bottom as for a full bust.) Cut along the side seam until you get to the armscye, pivot at the armscye, and then follow the armscye to the shoulder. Clip diagonally to the corners at the shoulder and underarm seams.

Spread the underarm corner to increase the width. If necessary, tuck the armscye curve along the outer edge to help it lie flat. To reduce the width of the back, move the underarm seam toward the center back, over the pattern.

Adjusting Darts

Bust darts should point to the bust points and end 1 in. away. For sizes 16 or larger, end the dart 1½ in. to 2 in. away from the point. Check the bust point by pin-fitting (see the sidebar on p. 28).

Shorten or lengthen darts that are in the right place but are not the right length. To do this, reposition the point and redraw the sewing line, blending to the original line (see the drawing below).

Move darts that are the right length but do not point to your bust point. To raise or lower the dart, draw a box around it and cut out the box. Reposition the box so that the dart points to the new bust point, and then true the side seam. You can also box in vertical darts and move them left to right.

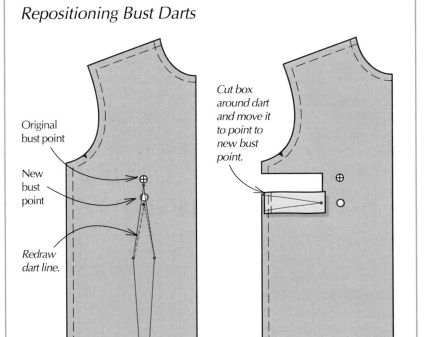

Repositioning Bust Darts

Original bust point

New bust point

Redraw dart line.

Cut box around dart and move it to point to new bust point.

Adjusting the Shoulder

There are three things that you might need to adjust for the shoulder—seam position, slope, and shoulder width. Check each of these when you pin-fit the pattern.

Seam Position The shoulder seam should follow your shoulder and be centered. It's common that you'll have to shift the seam to the front.

On the pattern front, mark where the new seam should be. Draw in the new sewing line, connecting the mark to the original shoulder seam near the neck. Draw in the new cutting line ⅝ in. away and cut away the triangle.

Add the triangle to the back shoulder seam and tape it in place. To compensate for the change, make sure to shift the center mark on the sleeve cap the same distance toward the front (see the top drawing at right).

Slope Use hinges to change the shoulder slope. Starting at the underarm, cut through the side seam 1 in. down from the armscye (see the bottom drawing at right). Cut along the sewing line at the armscye and the shoulder seam. Clip a diagonal hinge at both ends of the shoulder seam toward the corners without cutting through the edge. Raise or lower the shoulder seam the desired amount, and then tape in place. This adjustment raises or lowers the slope of the shoulder without changing the size of the armscye. Make the same adjustment for both front and back.

Width Adjust shoulder width using the same technique as for slope adjustment. Starting at the middle of the shoulder seam, cut through the seam allowance to the seamline. Cut toward the armscye along the shoulder seam, pivot, and follow the armscye until you get to the notch about two-thirds the way down. Clip to the edge at the shoulder seam without cutting through. Pull out the seam allowance to widen the shoulder; move it in to narrow the shoulder. Make the same adjustment for front and back.

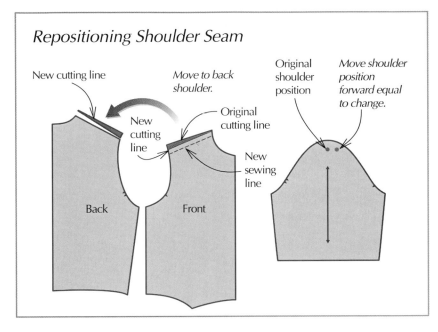

Repositioning Shoulder Seam

New cutting line

Move to back shoulder.

New cutting line

Original cutting line

Back

Front

New sewing line

Original shoulder position

Move shoulder position forward equal to change.

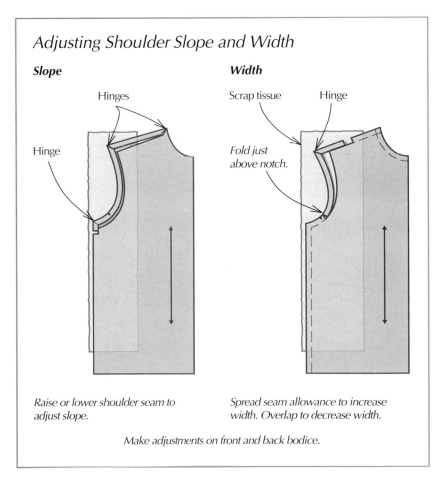

Adjusting Shoulder Slope and Width

Slope

Hinges

Hinge

Raise or lower shoulder seam to adjust slope.

Width

Scrap tissue

Hinge

Fold just above notch.

Spread seam allowance to increase width. Overlap to decrease width.

Make adjustments on front and back bodice.

Enhancing the Pattern

Fitting is not only about modifying the pattern to accommodate figure variations. Some areas of the blouse are improved by making minor changes to the pattern.

Simplify the pattern for difficult-to-sew fabrics or prints that are hard to match. For example, eliminate the back-yoke seam and pleats and seams that are not shaped.

Adjust the undercollar, cuffs, and collar stand to allow for turn-of-cloth. Making these adjustments helps the collar curve nicely around the neck and keeps the undercollar and cuff facings tucked under where they belong.

Cut full sleeves on the bias for graceful folds. Cutting on the bias also produces a more interesting effect on checks or plaids and eliminates the need to match the sleeve at the arm seam.

Another option for a cuffed sleeve with a continuous lap placket and pleats is to incorporate the cuff into the sleeve by extending the lines at the bottom. This "no-cuff" cuff eliminates the need to cut a separate cuff and uses a wider and longer placket than the original pattern. You also have the option of adding button loops or using small buttons and buttonholes.

Enhance any blouse with a separate, hidden placket. It's much easier to cut and sew than using a pattern that comes with an attached hidden closure. Also consider changing the patch pocket to a welt pocket.

These minor changes have a major impact on the finished blouse.

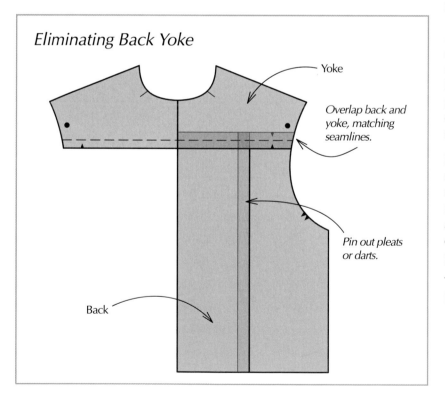

Eliminating Back Yoke

Yoke

Overlap back and yoke, matching seamlines.

Pin out pleats or darts.

Back

Eliminating Seams

If the blouse back has pleats, eliminate them. Extend the foldlines all the way to the bottom with a ruler, and then bring them together and pin.

To eliminate the back yoke, align the yoke and the blouse back (see the drawing on the facing page). Position the back and yoke seamlines on top of one another and pin together.

Eliminate center-back seams and side seams that are straight by overlapping the sewing lines and cutting as one piece.

Adjusting for Turn-of-Cloth

Modify the pattern for a more professional-looking collar, neck stand, and cuffs that curve nicely around the body. Reduce the outer edges of the undercollar by ⅛ in. This places the edge seam toward the undercollar and helps the upper collar curve under a bit at the edges. The neckline remains unchanged.

If you have a pattern for the full collar, make changes on half the collar and label it "undercollar." The unchanged half is the top collar. Draw lines inside the cutting lines of the outer edge and trim.

Don't separate the collar at the center back; just use it one-half at a time. Cut the upper collar by placing the center back on the fold and using that half of the collar. Cut the undercollar by using the undercollar half on the fold.

If the collar pattern is for half the collar, make a new pattern for the undercollar by placing the pattern tissue on top of the collar pattern and copying.

To reduce the upper curve of the neck stand, draw in a new outer edge ⅛ in. inside the original

For more graceful drape, cut sleeves on the bias. Use a triangle to mark in the new grainline on the sleeve. Line up a square side to the grainline and draw in the diagonal edge.

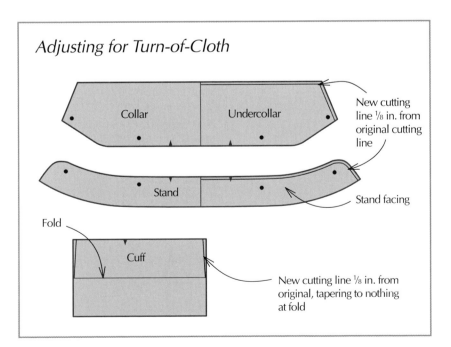

Adjusting for Turn-of-Cloth

Collar

Undercollar

New cutting line ⅛ in. from original cutting line

Stand

Stand facing

Fold

Cuff

New cutting line ⅛ in. from original, tapering to nothing at fold

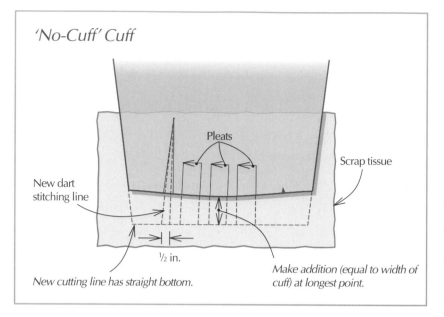

'No-Cuff' Cuff

Pleats

Scrap tissue

New dart stitching line

½ in.

New cutting line has straight bottom.

Make addition (equal to width of cuff) at longest point.

line. Extend side seams and pleat marks to the new cutting line. (You don't want to make the length adjustment from the normal adjustment line on the sleeve because it would not result in the elongated-cuff effect we are after, and the cuff opening would also be too short.)

Redraw the dart to be ½ in. wide at the new hem and to stay the same at the top.

Cut or tear the rectangle for the new placket. The length equals the total length of both dart seams. Keep the width at 1¼ in. if you are adding button loops at the opening (see pp. 94-95); otherwise, you can change the placket width to 2 in., which increases the overlap so you have more room to sew buttonholes.

After cutting the placket, use tracing paper to mark the pleats and the opening dart on the wrong side of the fabric.

cutting line using a see-through ruler. Redraw the upper curve on half the collar stand and label it "stand facing." The neck seam remains the same.

Reduce the sides of the cuff facing, which are adjacent to the notched cuff seam, by ⅛ in. Redraw the cutting lines on the cuff facing side only, tapering to nothing at the foldline.

Modifying the Cuff

For a different fashion look, make these few easy pattern changes to create a "no-cuff" cuff.

Extend the length of the pattern by the width of the finished cuff. First, mark in the new length. Cuffed sleeves usually have a contour hem, so take the longest length and draw a straight line parallel to the length-adjustment

Modifying the Front Closure

Change the look of the blouse by modifying the front closure. Add a hidden closure, as described below, or consider a decorative placket (see the sidebar on p. 102).

Hidden Closure You can add a hidden placket to any blouse pattern that doesn't have one. If your pattern already includes a hidden closure, use this method to avoid having to cut individual left and right fronts. (It's easier to control the front edge if you use a separate piece for the placket.)

Hidden-Front Closure

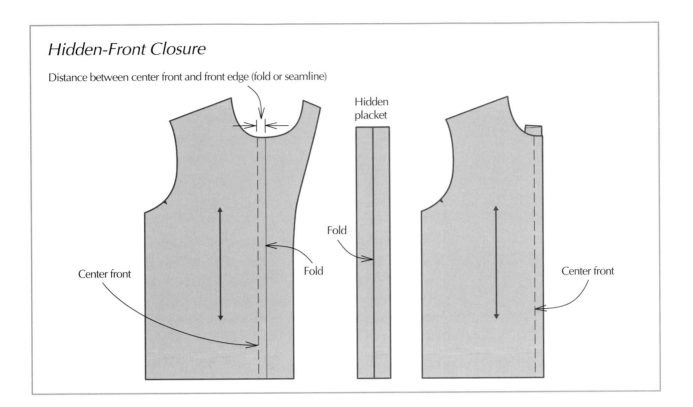

Distance between center front and front edge (fold or seamline)

Hidden placket

Fold

Fold

Fold

Center front

Center front

Fold the fabric with right sides together and use the left front pattern to cut both the left and right fronts. To cut the hidden-front placket, you must determine the correct width and length from your pattern:

Measure the distance between the center-front line and the finished front edge (either the front fold, or if there is a separate facing, the front sewing line).

Cut or tear a rectangle 4 times this measurement + 1 in. For example, if the distance between the center front and the front edge is ³/₄ in., the width equals 4 in. (³/₄ in. x 4 = 3 in. + 1 in. = 4 in.).

Cut the length equal to the length of the pattern front.

Fold the placket in half lengthwise and line up the fold to the front edge of the pattern. Cut the neckline following the pattern. Adjust the length to be 1¹/₂ in. shorter than the front edge.

Modifying the Pocket

It's easy to replace a patch pocket with a welt pocket. If you like the placement of the pocket, just redraw the marks. Draw a horizontal line connecting the two upper-corner placement marks. Using a see-through ruler, draw ¹/₂-in. lines at right angles to the pocket-placement line to mark the ends of the pocket opening.

Changing a Patch Pocket to a Welt Pocket

Draw line to connect patch-pocket top placement marks.

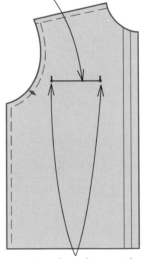

Draw ¹/₂-in. lines at right angle to placement lines.

Cutting and Marking

Accurate cutting and marking are the foundation for accurate sewing. First, you must true or straighten the crosswise grain of the fabric.

Straightening the Grain

Straighten the grain by tearing the fabric or pulling a thread.

Tearing the Fabric Clip into the selvage about 1 in. in from the cut edge and 1 in. beyond the selvage. If the fabric is cut noticeably shorter at one end, use that end.

Hold each side of the slit firmly and pull your hands away from each other to tear. Then press the tear ruffle flat.

Some fabrics won't tear. If the fabric grain starts distorting around the slit and resists tearing, you have a fabric that won't tear. Linens don't tear. Ribbon chiffon and other very lightweight fabrics that alternate between thick and lightweight stripes or areas of design and some corduroys should never be torn because they are unpredictable. The fabric may tear nicely at first, but when it meets resistance it starts to follow a lengthwise thread. For these fabrics, pull a thread to straighten the grain.

Pulling a Thread Clip into the selvage as explained for tearing the fabric. Find a crosswise thread in the clipped area and pull gently.

Pull the thread from selvage to selvage and cut along the pulled thread. The thread does not need to be removed, just shifted enough to provide a line for cutting. If the thread breaks and you lose your line, cut along the pulled thread as far as possible. Start pulling a new thread and continue to the end.

Cutting Basics

After straightening the edge, fold the fabric lengthwise, with the selvages together and the right side in. When the pattern layout shows one selvage folded in part of the way to the other selvage, make sure that the selvages are parallel to each other. The width of the folded area or the space between the selvages must be exactly the same throughout.

Lay out *all* the pattern pieces before you start cutting. Measure the grainline to the selvage edge or fold. Be meticulous about placing centerlines on the fold to avoid changing the width of the blouse or the angle of a neck facing. Use as few pins as possible (make sure they don't extend outside the cutting line), or use weights.

Cut flat, holding the pattern down with one hand as you cut with the other. Never lift the edge of the fabric to meet the scissors and never pull at the edge as you cut—if you do, as soon as you let go of the fabric it will spring back and you'll have a hunk of fabric missing at the edge. Never use pinking shears to cut; although it sounds good, pinking is inaccurate because the edges and corners are not clearly defined.

Notches mark match points to help you connect fabric sections when you sew. If you cut notches outward, it's easy to find them during the sewing process but it is more difficult to do and takes more time. On fabrics that fray easily, such as handkerchief linen, it's worth cutting notches outward. Alternatively, take *short* snips in the seam allowance. Taking short snips is especially important if using French seams or other enclosed seams (see pp. 51-52). Snip down the center of the notch and perpendicular to the edge.

For easy identification of blouse pieces, leave the pattern on cut pieces until you are ready to sew. Don't be a neatnik yet—save scraps of fabric to test stitches and interfacing and to practice buttonholes.

Measure carefully to ensure that the centerline is parallel to the selvage or fold.

Hold the pattern flat with one hand as you cut.

Cut snips rather than notches in seam allowances.

CUTTING INTERFACING

Cut interfacing using the facing pattern. It is not necessary to trim away the seam allowances for use on blouse-weight fabrics. To reduce bulk on outside corners, cut away the seam allowance diagonally.

Nonwoven fusible interfacing does not have a grain to follow, but many kinds have crosswise stretch with no lengthwise stretch. Cut these with the stable direction lengthwise to the pattern.

When the front or back facing is connected to the pattern front or back, the pattern companies seldom give you a separate interfacing pattern. Use the main pattern piece to cut the interfacing. The pattern indicates "cut interfacing to this line" with an arrow pointing to the foldline. The easy way to cut this piece is to fold the interfacing lengthwise, aligning the lengthwise edges exactly. Place the foldline of the pattern on top of the edges, so that the facings are on the interfacing and the blouse is not. Use this technique anytime you have to interface to a foldline.

CUTTING STRIPS FOR BIAS FACING AND PIPING

Mark diagonal lines to cut bias strips.

You can replace shaped facings on necklines and armholes using narrow bias facings (see pp. 65-66). To cut bias strips, find the straight of grain by tearing, and then measure an equal distance from the corner along each side. Be sure the fabric is square. Draw a diagonal line connecting both points. Cut additional bias strips using a clear ruler to mark the desired width.

Marking

There are other symbols besides notches along the sewing line that need to be transferred to the fashion fabric or interfacing, including large and small dots, squares, and triangles. If a piece is to be interfaced, mark the symbols on the interfacing and not the fashion fabric (except for notches, which should be made on both the interfacing and the fabric).

Most marks go on the wrong side of the fabric. Unstitched pleats and placement marks for patch pockets go on the right side. Snip-mark the center front, center back, and foldlines. Mark the center dot on the sleeve cap with a short snip.

There are several different marking tools available, but no single tool is perfect for all fabrics. Pencil and felt-tip markers are good for marking dots. Tracing paper and powder markers are good for lines. I use white whenever possible, with yellow as my second choice.

Refillable chalk markers dispense a fine line that is easily removed by light brushing or shaking of the garment. Marks made with erasable-ink markers must be removed with water. Air-erasable-ink marks disappear within 24 to 48 hours but can also be removed with water. The air-erasable pen available in a deep purple color is the one I trust the most for use on blouse-weight fabrics. An air-erasable tracing paper is also available. Marking pencils and

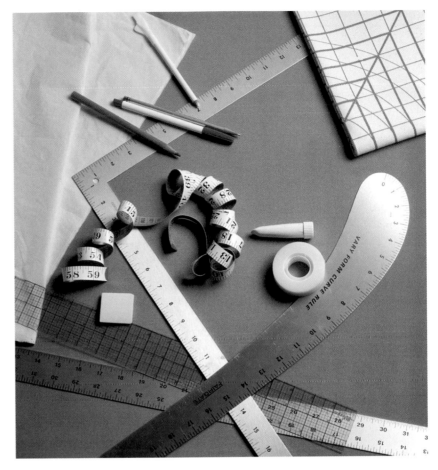

tailor's chalk can be waxy or chalky depending on the brand.

Use tracing paper and a tracing wheel to transfer lines. I prefer a spoked tracing wheel to the smooth type because it grips the surface and gives a better line. Wax or powder tracing paper is available. The wax type works best on thick fabrics and all weights of wool. The powder type is best on silky and lightweight fabrics.

Marking Dots Dots at a corner help you line up corners with different angles, or inside corners to outside corners. Mark these as dots by inserting a pin through the

If you start to join two pieces and the match points don't line up, either the two pieces don't belong together or a mark is wrong or missing. Before removing the pattern tissue from each blouse section, quickly look it over to be sure you have transferred all necessary marks.

Keep markings neat and to a minimum. Test the removal method, especially for light colors and thin fabrics. Remove marks before pressing to avoid setting the color.

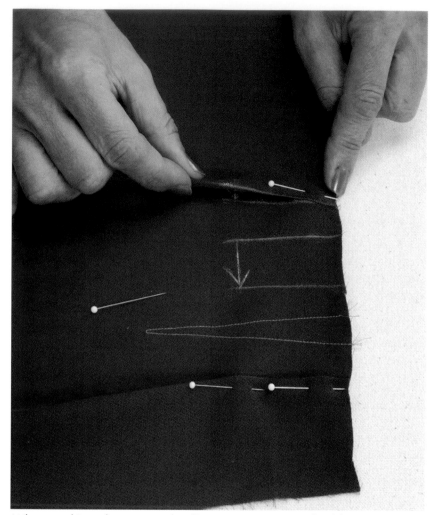

When marking pleats, trace the direction arrows onto the fabric, so you won't have to refer to the pattern later.

dot mark on the pattern tissue. Go through all layers. Lift the tissue and mark a dot on the wrong side of each layer. When pinning right sides together, mark where the pin enters and exits the fabric.

Use the pin and mark method for other marks such as squares and triangles. Insert the pin, and draw in a square or triangle at the pinhole. To distinguish between large and small dots, do the same

thing. This technique saves time in the long run, because you can easily identify match points referred to in the directions.

You can also mark dots along a seamline using short snips perpendicular to the edge and pointing to the dot. If you might confuse this snip with other snips along that edge, mark in a dot.

CUTTING AND MARKING SILKY FABRICS

The most difficult part about cutting silky fabrics is that they slide about as you lay out and cut the fabric. After straightening the cross grain, be sure to square the lengthwise and crosswise edges. The easiest and most accurate way to do this is to pin the silk to a gridded cutting board. Fold the fabric as recommended by the layout.

Line up the corner of the fabric to the corner of the grid. Pin the selvages to the line, and then pin the crosswise edge, moving away from the starting point. Smooth the fabric and lay out the pattern pieces. Use very fine pins or weights. Keep pins to a minimum and pin in the seam allowances whenever possible.

Be prudent with all marking. Substitute snips for marks whenever possible. Use a light touch. Mark the smallest dot and use the lightest color, especially when marking the right side. Use powder markers such as Chaco liner and air-erasable Mark-be-gone purple marker or tracing paper. Be sure to use powder-type tracing paper and powder pencils only. Waxy markers and pencils leave greasy marks when you iron over them. You can't always tell if there is any wax in marking pencils. Even a white pencil leaves oily marks behind, so always test before marking the actual fabric.

Marking Darts Mark the sewing line on the wrong side using the appropriate tracing paper and tracing wheel. Apply firm pressure and trace only once along the sewing line—going back and forth over a line with the tracing wheel creates a confusion of lines that are inaccurate and impossible to follow. Trace a line across the point to identify it clearly.

Another option is to mark in only the dots along the sewing line and connect the dots as you sew. This method works fine for simple darts with straight sides, but for darts with curved seams it's more accurate to mark using tracing paper.

Marking Pleats Check the sewing direction for the point of reference. Do you bring the lines together on the wrong side or the right side of the fabric? For unstitched pleats you usually pin—and therefore mark—from the right side. Use white or air-erasable tracing paper to mark the foldlines.

Marking Buttonholes Mark machine-made buttonholes after the blouse is completed (on the right side of the blouse).

4 | *The Best Sewing Techniques*

Patterns present a basic, standard method to do a technique, but the directions and seam finishes recommended on the pattern are not always the best choice for sewing lightweight fabrics. For example, if you press the seam open and zigzag the edges on a bottom-weight fabric, you get a nice finish. If you do this with a blouse-weight fabric, you get a chewed-up edge that forms a ridge. The techniques in this chapter are mindful of using lightweight fabrics and sewing washable garments. They are not just for blouses—use them whenever you sew a lightweight or a silky fabric.

Use this chapter to supplement or override the pattern directions. Some techniques are changed just slightly to make them easier and more manageable. Other techniques replace the standard directions with a technique from ready-to-wear that produces professional results.

Use patterns you like in a different way. Make simple changes like using a purchased knit collar instead of the pattern for a casual look. Add piping to seams or edges. Replace facings with bindings for pastel-colored fabrics and sheers. Create versatile pieces for your wardrobe by making simple changes to the pattern. Adding long side slits to a blouse enables you to wear it creatively. Wear it belted or tucked in, or tie the slits at one side to create a wonderful side drape. For a truly reversible vest or sleeveless blouse, use buttonholes on both sides of the opening and attach buttons to a grosgrain ribbon to be usable from either side.

The techniques in this chapter take you past the beginner's stage. For example, welt pockets are not for beginners, but they are classic details that are worth the extra effort. Try them when you want to take on a bit of a challenge. As you sew more blouses you add new techniques to your sewing repertoire. Finally, use these techniques to sew the quintessential silk blouse, which no wardrobe is complete without.

Before You Sew

The way you perform basic steps makes the task easier and more efficient. Pin placement and the pinning sequence help you control the seam, especially when pinning together two completely different edges.

When two seam allowances that get sewn together have different-shaped corners at each end, match the cut edges and the ends at the sewing line. The outermost corners will not match, but you will get a matching edge along the seam where it counts.

Good work habits contribute to the quality of every project. Work in a well-lit area and position yourself in front of the sewing machine, centered to the presser foot. Have your pin holder and thread snipper close to hand. Follow the guides to the right of the needle whenever possible.

Pinning Seams

Pin seams with right sides together at regular intervals. The pins should be perpendicular to the edge, with the heads extending off the fabric (see the photo below).

The cut edges must line up. Match ends, notches, and other match points, and then add more pins in between as needed. Straight seams on stable fabrics require a few pins. On slippery fabrics or when pinning edges together with different shapes, such as sleeves to bodices, or collars to necklines, pin at frequent intervals. Remove pins as you come to them; never press over them.

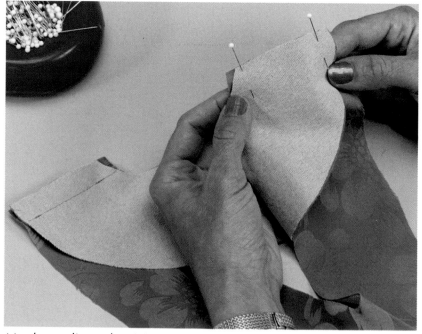

Match seamlines when joining pieces that have different-shaped corners.

Sewing Basics

- Press all seams as you sew.

- Keep the bulk of the fabric to the left whenever possible.

- To sew a straight seam, follow the guidelines on your machine. If your machine doesn't have guidelines, mark your own lines a measured distance from the needle.

- Sew seams end to end unless otherwise directed.

- Pay extra attention to dot marks and other match points to avoid having to rip out stitches. Sometimes you have to sew *between* the dots, sometimes *to* the dot and other times *through* the dot. These are three completely different things.

- Hold the thread at the start of your seam to avoid messy starts.

- Backstitch only two to three stitches for regular seams. The best place to backstitch is about 1/2 in. in from the edge.

CONSTRUCTION SEQUENCE

Use the following general construction sequence for sewing all types of blouses. There is some overlap because there are so many style variations. A single blouse will not have all these details; for example, your blouse may or may not have a center-back seam, a yoke, or cuffs. As you follow the sewing sequence, just skip the steps that do not apply to your blouse.

1. Prepare the fabric and interfacing for sewing (p. 18).

2. Compare your body measurements to the pattern and pin-fit (pp. 26-28).

3. Adjust the pattern where necessary, such as:
- increasing the length (p. 29)
- adjusting for a full bust (p. 31)
- repositioning darts (p. 32)

4. Cut and mark the fabric (pp. 38-43).

5. Fuse interfacing (p. 55).

6. Sew and fuse faced facing (pp. 64-65).

7. Sew center-back seam. Sew darts, pleats, or gathers (pp. 61-63).

8. Sew pockets (pp. 56-60).

9. Sew and attach hidden-front placket (pp. 101-102).

10. Sew shoulder seams:
- shirt-type yoke (pp. 77-78)
- blouse-type yoke (pp. 80-82)

11. Sew and attach the collar (pp. 68-75).

12. Sew and attach the neck facing (or bias binding), or use ribbing as a neckline finish (pp. 65-67).

13. Sew sleeve plackets (pp. 87-91).

14. Attach sleeves to blouse (if flat-sleeve application, pp. 83-84).

15. Sew blouse side seams and sleeve side seams.

16. Attach sleeves to blouse in the round (pp. 84-86).

17. Sew cuffs to sleeves (pp. 92-93).

18. Hem blouse (pp. 98-100).

19. Mark and sew buttonholes; mark button placement and sew on blouse (pp. 103-105).

20. Attach shoulder pads (p. 79).

Basic Construction Techniques and Terms

You need to understand the following basic techniques and sewing terms in order to be able to follow the sewing directions.

Directional Sewing

Directional sewing involves sewing or staystitching a seam following a particular direction. Curved or angled seams are off-grain and easily stretched during the sewing process. Sew with the grain whenever possible. You can tell the best direction to sew by running your finger along the cut fabric edge. Sew in the direction that smooths the threads together and down. Sewing in the direction that pulls and separates the threads away from the edge is more likely to result in a stretched edge.

Pattern directions routinely recommend staystitching off-grain edges prior to sewing the seams together. This is time-consuming and unnecessary. Rather than staystitching individual edges, use directional stitching to sew the seams together whenever possible. I staystitch only when the edge needs to be clipped, to stabilize an edge before attaching binding, or to stabilize a narrow edge and press it under.

To sew smoothly rounded corners, keep the needle down, lift the presser foot, and pivot the fabric.

Curves

It's easy to lose sight of the $5/8$-in. sewing line when sewing curves. Here are some tips to make it easier: If you have the option, sew with the needle automatically stopping in the down position. Use a shorter stitch length and be sure not to stretch the fabric. Start sewing on the $5/8$-in. mark and keep the seam allowance to the right of the presser foot a constant width; do this instead of trying to follow the mark. Sharp curves require pivoting slightly and frequently.

Corners

To pivot at corners, stop with the needle down, raise the presser foot, and turn the fabric with the needle in place. Lower the presser foot and sew following the adjacent seam.

For accurate inside corners be sure to mark the pivot points. To sew, shorten the stitch length as you approach the corner (about 1 in. away). Stop with the needle in the fabric. Pivot at the corner and sew another inch before resetting the stitch length.

Stitches

The straight stitch is the most basic and widely used stitch. Here are some other basic stitches used during the various stages of sewing blouses:

Staystitch A stitch sewn through a single layer of fabric using a regular stitch length to stabilize edges that are off-grain. Sew $1/8$ in. from the seamline in the seam allowance. For example, for a $5/8$-in. seam allowance staystitch at $1/2$ in.

Reinforce Stitch Use a shorter stitch length (18 to 20 stitches per inch) placed on the seamline at points of strain. Reinforce stitches are always used on inside corners that must be clipped, such as V-necklines.

Easestitch A long stitch through a single layer used to reduce the length of the seam between two points. Leave thread tails at both ends to pull up ease and to distribute fullness as evenly as possible. The eased area is smooth and slightly rounded near the seam.

Gathering Stitch A gathering stitch is made in the same way as an ease stitch, but with gathers you distribute larger areas of fullness evenly. Leave thread tails at both ends to gather fabric. Two parallel rows of stitching give you the best control. Sew one row at $3/8$ in. and one at $5/8$ in.

Baste Stitch A long machine stitch used to hold two or more layers of fabric together temporarily for stitching or fitting.

Topstitch Stitching done from the right side of the fabric. The stitch can be near the edge

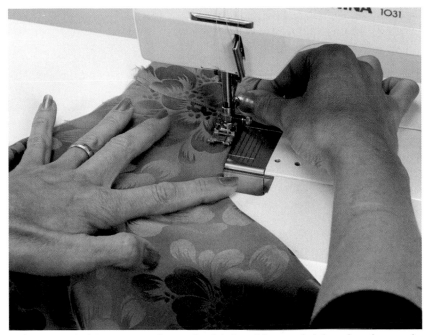

When topstitching curves, frame the fabric with your left hand and smooth it away from the needle as you sew to avoid shifting the top layer of fabric and creating diagonal folds.

(edgestitch), $1/4$ in. in, or any other place indicated by the instructions.

Slipstitch A hand-sewing stitch used to join a folded edge to a seam or flat surface. Slide the needle under the folded edge and then pick up a thread of the underlying fabric.

Whipstitch A hand-sewing stitch used to join two finished edges or to secure fasteners such as snaps and hooks and eyes. Insert the needle at a right angle to the fabric edge or fastener edge, picking up a few threads as you pass it through. Repeat, sewing over the edge of the fabric or fastener. Use short, close-together stitches for securing fasteners and long stitches for basting welt pockets.

Finish Stitch Stitch $1/4$ in. from a raw edge, then turn in along the stitching and stitch close to the fold.

SPECIAL TECHNIQUES FOR SEWING SILKY FABRICS

"Silky" refers to any fabric that is slippery to cut and sew. All silk fabrics are not silky. Silk gabardine and silk taffeta are very stable. A fabric is silky because of a combination of fiber, weave, and weight or drape. Some common silkies are silk or polyester crêpe de chine, silk or polyester jacquards, lightweight rayon fabrics, and some challis. Slippery fabrics require extra attention when cutting and sewing, and they are more sensitive to the sewing techniques you use. All the techniques in this book are appropriate for silkies. Use these additional guidelines for best results.

• Use extra-fine silk pins or fine pleating pins, and pin at close intervals.

• Before you begin, check the stitch length and quality. Change the needle and thread type or size if necessary (see pp. 21-22).

• Use silk thread for beautiful, lustrous buttonholes that blend perfectly with the blouse fabric.

• Use a shorter stitch length of 14 to 20 stitches to the inch. If the stitch is too short for the fabric, the seam will stretch and look wavy; if the stitch is too long, the seam will look puckered. Use taut sewing when the seam is on the straight of grain to prevent puckering and help keep the edges together. To do this, pull the fabric in front of and behind the needle as you sew. Move with the fabric as it feeds back. Sew bias, curved, and off-grain seams without pulling at the fabric.

• Don't backstitch if it causes the fabric to pucker. When the stitchline ends mid-seam, lock in the stitch by sewing in place or turning the fabric around to sew in the direction you started.

• Use the thread tails to pull the fabric back when you start to sew. If your fabric sinks into the throat plate at the start of the seam, use a piece of paper as a lead for sewing the seam. Start sewing on the paper, overlap the start of the seam to the paper, and continue sewing onto the cloth without interrupting the stitch.

• If you have the choice, a straight-stitch foot and a straight-stitch throat plate will always give you a better straight stitch. The straight-stitch throat plate has a smaller hole for the needle to go through, so a lightweight fabric is less likely to sink into it. You can simulate this by taping over the hole of the zigzag throat plate that comes with zigzag machines. Be sure to avoid taping over the feed dogs.

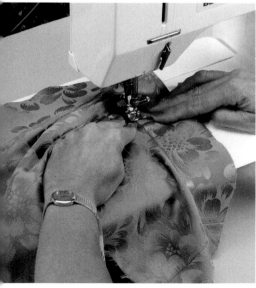

Pull the fabric away from the needle as you understitch.

Understitch A regular-length straight stitch used to keep facing rolled to the inside of the garment. Trim, clip, and press the seam allowance toward the facing. Sew the seam allowance to the facing. Stitch right side up and on the facing, $\frac{1}{8}$ in. from the seam.

Understitching is a wonderful technique that originated in ready-to-wear. When done properly it results in a smooth, flat edge seam that falls into the right position for pressing. If done improperly, the edge looks erratic and the facing shows along the edge.

Here are some things to watch for when understitching:

• Be sure to catch the entire seam allowance—clipped sections sometimes flip back. Check and adjust the seam allowance as you sew.

• Don't sew more than $\frac{1}{8}$ in. away from the seam; otherwise, the seam will pucker.

• If the facing is not pressed completely away from the seam and you sew over it, the facing will show on the outside. To avoid this problem, press the seam with your fingertips by pulling the fabric away from the needle from both sides as you sew.

Seams and Seam Finishes

All seams look neat when you first sew them. On blouses and other frequently washed garments it's important to use seam finishes that stay neat. Most of the following finishes keep the seam allowances together and enclose or stitch down the raw edges. They require less maintenance and are appropriate for all blouse-weight fabrics, including silkies.

Standard Seams

The standard seam is created by sewing two pieces of fabric together with a straight stitch and then pressing the seam allowance open. Finish-stitch each seam for a neat look and to prevent raveling. Use the standard seam when the seam must be pressed open because of another detail, such as a center-back seam connected to a back facing, or side seams with slits.

Double-Stitched Seams

For a double-stitched seam, first stitch a conventional straight-stitch seam. Line up the left side of the presser foot to the straight stitch and stitch again in the seam allowance to prevent raveling; use a zigzag stitch, a three-step zigzag, or any of the edge-finishing stitches available on your machine. Trim the seam allowance close to the second row of stitches.

Always do a test. Some stitches pucker or chew up the seam. If the second stitch squeezes the fabric together, try reducing the stitch width or use a different stitch. The second stitch could also be done on the serger.

Self-Enclosed Seams

Self-enclosed seams are perfect for lightweight fabrics, such as sheer fabrics, lightweight silks, polyesters, linens, and cottons, and they endure repeated laundering. Cut edges are completely enclosed in the seam. The French seam and bound seam are virtually interchangeable.

French Seam Stitch the seam with wrong sides together, $3/8$ in. in from the edge (see the drawing at left on p. 52).

Press the seam open. Fold right sides together, with the seamline exactly on the edge, and press again. Trim the seam to $1/8$ in.

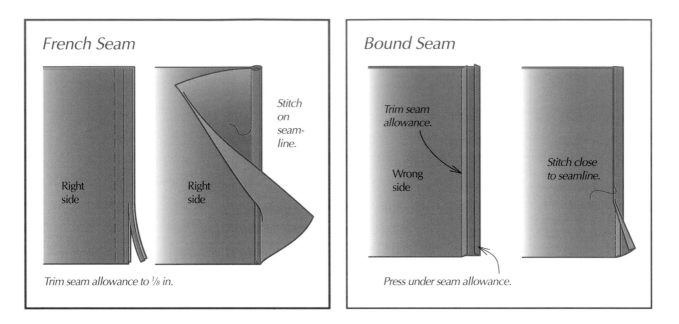

French Seam

Right side

Right side

Stitch on seam-line.

Trim seam allowance to ⅛ in.

Bound Seam

Trim seam allowance.

Wrong side

Stitch close to seamline.

Press under seam allowance.

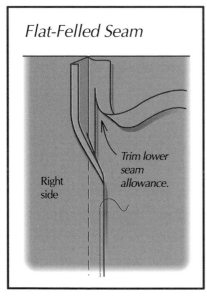

Flat-Felled Seam

Right side

Trim lower seam allowance.

Stitch on the seamline, which is now ¼ in. in from the fold. Press the seam to one side.

Polyester silkies and sheers are difficult to press, and sometimes unravel easily. As an option with these fabrics, stitch the seam with wrong sides together, ⅜ in. in from the edge. Stitch again in the seam ⅛ in. away from the first stitch. Trim next to the stitch. (Alternatively, you can serge using a ⅜-in. seam allowance.)

Press to one side. Fold right sides together with the seamline on the edge and press again. Stitch ¼ in. in from the fold. Press the seam to one side.

Bound Seam Sew a ⅝-in. seam with right sides together. Trim one seam allowance to between ⅛ in. and ¼ in. (see the top drawing at right). Press under the untrimmed edge ¼ in. Then press again, enclosing the trimmed edge.

Stitch the folded edge, as close as possible to the seamline. Press the seam to one side.

Flat-Felled Seam A flat-felled seam looks great on both sides. The traditional method has the double-stitched seam on the right side (as explained below). The other option is to follow the same directions but start sewing with the fabric right sides together. For the last step, you sew from the right side ¼ in. away from the seam. This way the double-stitched seam is on the wrong side, and you have a ¼-in. topstitched seam on the right side.

The flat-felled seam is popular on men's shirts and classic denim jeans and jackets. Use it anytime you want a secure seam that stays in place.

Stitch the seam with wrong sides together, ⅝ in. from the edge. Press the seam allowance to one side and trim the lower seam allowance to ⅛ in.

Press under ¼ in. on the untrimmed seam allowance, enclosing the lower one. Press the seam flat and pin, concealing the trimmed edge. Edgestitch on the fold.

Trimming, Grading, Clipping, and Notching

Some seams require extra techniques. Faced edges and seams on outer edges, such as necklines, collars, and cuffs, must be trimmed or graded, clipped or notched to reduce bulk. Do one or all of these to the seam allowance to achieve a flat, smooth finish.

Trimming Trim seam allowances to ¼ in. or ⅜ in. Trim outside corners on enclosed seams such as collars diagonally. Leave a ⅛-in. seam allowance across the point. Then trim again, tapering the seam allowance to the point.

Trim away the corners of the shoulder seam allowance formed by sewing the neck seam. Cut next to the stitching at the shoulder seam and neck seam.

Grading To eliminate bulk, grade seams by trimming seam allowances to graduated lengths. On a simple seam, cut the facing seam allowance to ¼ in. and the garment seam to ⅜ in. (On a lightweight blouse, grading is not necessary.)

The more layers there are in the fabric seam, the more necessary grading becomes (even on lightweight fabrics). On a blouse with a collar and a facing, there are at least four seam allowances in the neck seam. On this seam, trim the facing to ⅛ in. and each next layer ⅛ in. wider. The widest seam allowance is always uppermost when you wear the blouse.

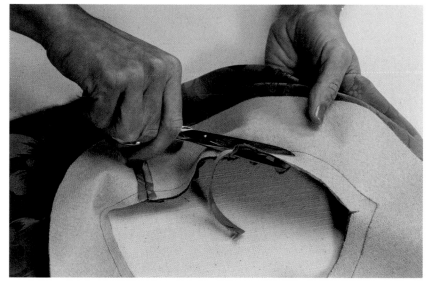

Grade thin fabrics by laying scissors flat, beveling the seam.

Another way to grade on thin fabrics or multilayers is to bevel the seam. Cut with your wrist rotated toward you, with the scissors as flat as possible to the cloth, to trim the uppermost layer shorter than the next.

Clipping Clipping is necessary on inside corners and curves. On inside curves, use the tips of your scissors to clip to the stitchline, but not through it, at frequent intervals. Clipping permits the seam allowance to spread and lie flat when pressed toward the body of the garment.

Notching Notches help outside curves lie flat. After trimming the seam allowance, turn the curved seam right side out. If ripples form in the seam allowance, use pinking shears to cut V-shaped wedges at equal intervals. Remember that clips are slits that allow the edge to spread, whereas notches are wedges cut away from the seam allowance that allow the edge to draw in.

Clipping and notching are not always necessary on regular seams that get double-stitched or pressed open. Having to do so depends on the sharpness of the curve and the type of fabric you are using. First, see if you can press the seam in the direction you want, and then clip or notch the seam only where it won't lie flat.

Pressing

Pressing is not the same as ironing. You iron clothing to remove wrinkles; you press as you sew to embed the stitches and to shape seams. Pressing is an important step at all stages of the sewing process.

General Pressing Guide

When pressing, use a gentle up-and-down motion—don't wiggle the iron around, or you'll create wrinkles. Lift the iron to move to another area, and let the fabric cool before you move it. Don't press over pins. Do as much pressing from the wrong side as possible. Top pressing on some fabrics causes shine; on these fabrics, use a press cloth or Teflon iron soleplate.

The first step to all pressing is to seal the seam by pressing the seam flat; this embeds the stitches. The next step is to press the seam open or to one side, depending on the type of seam you are sewing. Press vertical darts toward the center front and back darts toward the center back. Press horizontal darts up or down depending on the pattern directions. Press double-stitched and self-enclosed side seams and shoulder seams toward the front. Press the facing shoulder seams either open or toward the back.

Tools you'll need for pressing include:

- a well-padded ironing board

- a steam iron that releases a burst of steam

- a point presser

- a seam roll

- a sleeve board

- a tailor's ham

- two press cloths, one for fusing and one for top pressing

- a Teflon soleplate

Seal all seams by pressing them flat, embedding the stitch.

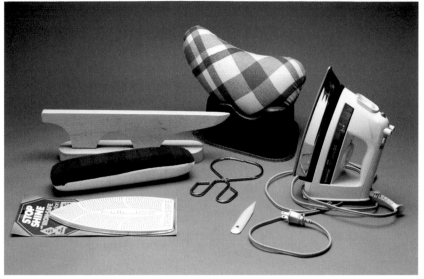

When pressing polyester fabrics that don't take a crease, use a ceramic tile as a pressing block.

Tools for pressing include (clockwise from left) a soleplate, seam roll, point presser, tailor's ham, and steam iron. Shown at center are two tools for turning collars.

Fusing Interfacing

Use a press cloth and fuse following the manufacturer's directions. Most directions call for using steam with a dry press cloth. Every iron is different, so the directions are only a starting point. If your iron doesn't steam much, you'll need to spray the press cloth with water to provide the heat and moisture necessary for adhesion. Iron temperatures vary, too. Always do a test. Use the coolest temperature possible that will steam without spitting out the water. Too hot an iron will shrink the interfacing and pucker or scorch the fashion fabric.

The first step is to align the interfacing (adhesive side down) over the wrong side of the fabric. Hold the iron 1 in. above the surface and steam the entire area. This will shrink some interfacing prior to fusing to the fabric.

However, on silky and drapey fabrics, the best way to fuse is by placing the silk on top of the interfacing, which makes it easier to align the edges.

Use an up-and-down motion to steam-baste the interfacing. Start at one end and touch the iron to the interfacing for three seconds. Never drag the iron. If the interfacing edge goes out beyond the fabric edge, trim the interfacing so it doesn't stick to your ironing board.

To finish fusing, always use a press cloth. The length of time for this step varies depending on the interfacing type, but 12 seconds is average. After fusing from the wrong side in an overlapping motion, fuse again from the right side using another press cloth. Keep a separate press cloth for top pressing because the resin builds up on the cloth during the fusing process. The buildup will eventually spot the fashion fabric during normal pressing.

On silky fabrics, fuse the interfacing with the fabric on top.

Sewing Pockets

Pockets may be applied to the surface of the blouse, as in patch pockets, or inserted in a slash, as in welt pockets. They may be functional, decorative, or both. Whichever type you use, they should lie flat over the body and not pull or distort around the edges.

Patch Pockets

Patch pockets are often used on blouses as a decorative detail. If you opt for patch pockets on your blouse, placement must be flattering and pockets must be perfect. Curved corners look great but require special attention. Follow these steps for beautiful pockets with identical curves.

Cut a strip of interfacing $1/2$ in. wider than the pocket facing so that it extends past the foldline. Fuse the interfacing. Press under a $1/4$-in. hem at the top edge **(1)**.

Cut a cardboard template from your pocket pattern (you can buy a metal template, but it's just as easy to make your own). Trim away seam allowances; do not include the top facing or hem.

Turn the upper edge to the outside along the foldline. Sew across the ends of the pocket facing, catching the turned-up hem in the stitching **(2)**. Trim seams, stopping $1/4$ in. above the facing hem.

Turn the pocket right side out. Fit the template into the corners on the wrong side. Press all straight sides first, then press curves toward the template **(3)**. Trim the seam allowances to $1/4$ in. **(4)**.

Stitch down the upper hem from the right side. Hold the hem fold in place using fusible web or double-sided tape. Pin the pocket into position and edgestitch (5). Reinforce upper corners by reducing the stitch length or by stitching a triangle.

On soft fabrics and silkies, hand-baste the pocket facing to the blouse front to avoid a droopy look. Sew from the inside of the blouse and catch only the hem layer of the pocket.

1 Fuse a strip of interfacing on the pocket facing. (Shown at right is the template made from the pocket pattern.)

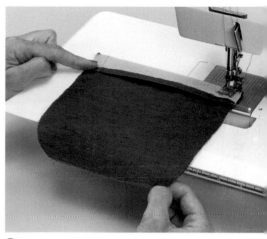

2 Sew the ends of the pocket facing, catching the hem allowance.

3 Fit the template into the corners and press the seam allowances.

4 Trim the seam allowances to ¼ in.

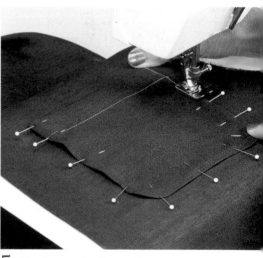

5 Pin the pocket in position and edgestitch.

fusible interfacing, such as Sofknit or Sofbrush. Cut a 3-in.-wide rectangle of interfacing equal in length to the width of the pocket opening plus 3 in. Center the interfacing on the wrong side of the blouse where the pocket goes and fuse in place. Use the pattern to mark the pocket placement. Then use $1/2$-in. tape to mark the rectangle (the sides of the tape define the sewing line) **(1)**.

To prepare the pocket, cut, or preferably tear, a rectangle from the blouse fabric to the following dimensions: the width of the finished pocket plus $1 1/2$ in.; two times the finished length plus 4 in. Draw a placement line on the pocket (see photo 1). Measure from the bottom edge 1 in. more than the finished length. For a pocket 4 in. long, draw a line 5 in. up from lower edge.

Position the pocket to the front with right sides together. Match the pocket placement line to the lower side of the rectangle. Make sure the pocket is centered vertically. Checkpoint: the longer pocket section should be toward the shoulders.

Stitch around the taped welt box **(2)**. You must have a continuous stitch around the corners. Start sewing near the lower left corner. Use a stitch length of 2 for the horizontal seams, but shorten the stitch length to about 1.5 near and around the corners. Overlap the stitch at the end instead of backstitching.

Remove the tape and mark the middle of the opening **(3)**. Slash the welt opening between the stitching. It is important to cut in the middle and to cut completely to the corner stitching **(4)**.

Welt Pockets

Welt pockets are a beautiful addition to a blouse, and they always hold their shape. These pockets are also known as bound pockets because the pocket material is used to bind off the pocket edges. Sew the welts using the same fabric as the blouse or a complementary fabric. The method described here is the easiest way to sew welt pockets because both the pocket and the welt are formed from a single rectangle of fabric.

Welt pockets are easier to make if you interface the blouse around the welt opening. Use lightweight,

1 *Mark the sewing line on the blouse with ½-in. tape, and then draw a placement line on the pocket fabric.*

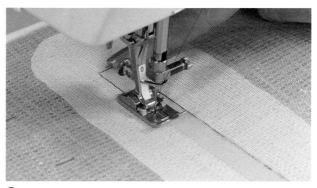

2 *Stitch around the taped welt box.*

On the right side, press all four sides of the pocket toward the opening (**5**). Push the pocket fabric through the opening. Then press both ends under so the seam is now on the edge and the pocket fabric is completely turned under (**6,** p. 60).

To form welts, wrap the pocket fabric *tightly* around, encasing the slashed edge. Press or pin in place (being careful not to press over the pins) (**7,** p. 60).

Sew the lower welt first. Start at either corner on the right side. Instead of backstitching shorten the stitch length to zero. Spread the welt seam with your fingers until the original stitching around the rectangle is visible. Stitch on top of the original stitching.

Before sewing the upper welt, fold the pocket down about ½ in. above the opening. Press, then pin to hold. Sew the upper welt from the right side, the same as you did for the lower welt (**8,** p. 60). Stitch on top of the original stitching through all thicknesses. This step will also hold the fold in place.

On the right side, adjust the welts so that the corners are square and the welts are just touching. Pin and machine-baste to hold in

3 *Remove the tape and mark the middle of the rectangle.*

4 *Slash the welt opening between the stitching and cut to the corners.*

5 *On the right side, press the pocket fabric toward the opening.*

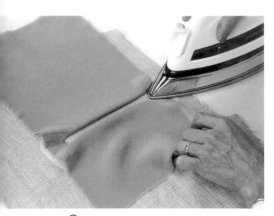

6 *On the wrong side, press the end seams under.*

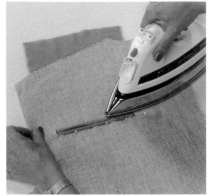

7 *After encasing the slashed edges, press or pin the welts in place.*

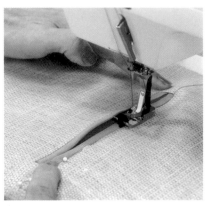

8 *Sew the upper welt from the right side.*

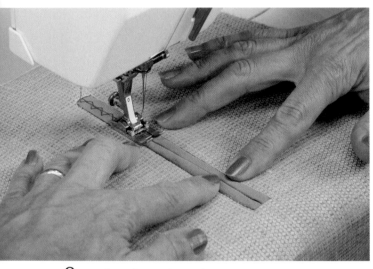

9 *Machine-baste the welts in position using a zigzag stitch.*

10 *Stitch around the pocket, catching the triangle in the stitching at both ends.*

For delicate fabrics, hand-baste the welts using a silk thread or a rayon embroidery thread. Loosely whipstitch the edges together.

position. Use the longest and widest zigzag setting you have (length 5 and width 5 on most machines) **(9)**.

On the backside, pin the pocket edges together. Stitch around the pocket, starting above the triangle. Catch the triangle in your stitching at both ends **(10)**. If the lower edges are a different length, trim away the excess. Remove the zigzag stitches.

Single-Welt Option Follow the directions for the standard welt up to where you slash the welt

opening. Then fold the welt fabric around the lower welt to form one 1/2-in. wide welt. Press to hold, and sew the lower welt as explained previously.

Press the remaining pocket layer toward the bottom of the blouse. On the outside, adjust the single welt so the corners are square and the single welt just covers the facing seam. Baste to hold, and stitch around the pocket as for the standard welt.

Shaping the Blouse

There are different ways to shape fabric so that it will conform to and flatter your figure. Use darts, pleats, and gathers to create shape and fullness.

Darts at the bust or waist indicate a close fit that conforms to your figure. Pleats on a shoulder or sleeve build more ease into that area. Each pleat forms a vertical fold that looks soft and lies flat even in a crisp fabric. Gathers are another way to control fullness in an area. Used on a crisp fabric, gathers stand away from the body. On a silky fabric, the same gathers create a soft billowy shape. Pleats and gathers are interchangeable in many cases.

together with pin heads toward the dart point. Check on the reverse side to make sure the pins follow the lines.

Stitch from the wide end to the point, angling the fabric so that by the time you reach the point you will sew off the fabric (**1**). Sew off the edge of cloth. Do not cut the thread. Raise the presser foot and pull the dart toward you. Lower the presser foot and stitch again in the dart. This secures the thread ends and replaces backstitching (**2**).

To ensure that the sewing lines stay together, position the dart under the presser foot and manually insert the sewing needle into the cloth before removing the first pin to sew.

Darts

Accurate dart placement, marking, and sewing are necessary for a professional look. It is very important that darts taper gradually at the tip. If when you sew to the dart tip you are $1/8$ in. away from the folded edge, it's better to lengthen the dart than to suddenly scoot off the fabric, which would cause a dimple at the point. When you lengthen a dart on one side, you also need to lengthen the corresponding dart on the other side.

Here's a simple way to sew accurate darts and avoid the dimples. Begin by folding the dart lengthwise. Pin sewing lines

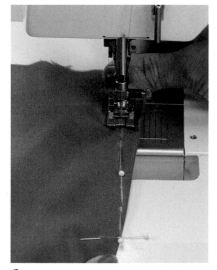

1 *Stitch the dart from the wide end to the point, angling the fabric.*

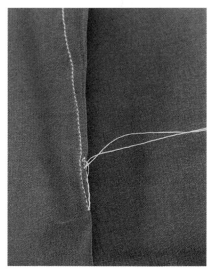

2 *Secure the thread ends by stitching the end of the dart again.*

Pleats

Pleats on blouses most frequently have soft vertical folds; they are easy to sew. To avoid confusion about the direction of the folds, be sure to mark the direction arrows on the pattern right onto the fashion fabric (see the photo on p. 42). Most of the time you work from the right side of the fabric. Check the pattern directions, and mark the side indicated.

To form pleats, bring one foldline to the other in the direction of the arrow. Pin foldlines together. To head off trouble, make sure the cut edges are also perfectly aligned before you sew. If they are not aligned, the pleats will not lie properly.

Baste pleats along the top edge using a $\frac{1}{2}$-in. seam allowance. This will hold them in place until that seam is sewn.

Sew darts that taper at both ends in two steps. Begin at the center and sew toward each point. Overlap the stitching at the center instead of backstitching.

Baste pleats in position using a $\frac{1}{2}$-in. seam allowance.

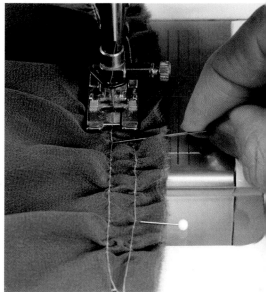

1 *Pin right sides of pieces together, distributing and pinning the gathers. Control gathers by wrapping the thread ends around the pins.*

2 *Baste along the sewing line, using a pin to adjust the gathers.*

Gathers

Use the following steps to sew gathers that are evenly distributed every time:

Stitch two parallel rows of basting stitches between the end marks. Stitch at ³⁄₈ in. and ⁵⁄₈ in. Make sure not to backstitch, and leave tails of threads at both ends so you can pull on them.

Pin the stitched edge to the matching garment piece with right sides together. Place pins perpendicular to the cut edge and avoid pinning through the stitches. Pin notches, dots, and any marks that belong together. Secure the threads at one end. Now pull the unsecured thread ends until the gathered edge is the same length as the ungathered edge (1). Distribute gathers evenly between the pins and add additional pins.

Baste along the sewing line, gathered side up. You can make additional improvements in the ease distribution by using a long pin or needle to adjust gathers as you sew (2). Check the underside for unwanted folds. If there's a problem, the basting is easily removed. If it looks good, sew again with a regular-length stitch.

Neckline Finishes

Shaped facings are used to finish necklines, armholes, and contour hems. As a rule, use fusible interfacing to stabilize facing pieces. You can also finish necklines and armholes by applying bias facings or adding knitted ribbing.

Shaped Facings

Cut the front and back facings out of the blouse fabric and the fusible interfacing. Fuse the interfacing layer to the wrong side of the front and back facings. Sew the front facing to the back facing at the shoulder seams only. Trim the shoulder seams to ¼ in. and press them open.

Turn and stitch the outer edge of the facing (it's easiest to do this if you staystitch ¼ in. from the outer edge). Press the seam allowance

To bind the outer facing edge, use ⅝-in.-wide bias-tricot trim. Center the tricot along the seam edge so that it curls around the fabric and encloses the raw edge. Use a zigzag stitch to sew in place.

to the wrong side along the stitch line and edgestitch with the right side of the facing up, starting at a shoulder seam. You can also finish the facing by serging, binding the outer edge with bias tricot, or using the faced-facing technique.

To attach the facing, pin and sew it to the blouse neck seam with right sides together. Trim and clip seam allowances.

Press the seam allowances toward the facing and understitch. Turn the facing to the inside and press the neckline. Tack the facing to the shoulder seams.

Faced Facings

The faced-facing technique allows you to finish the edge of the facing as you apply the interfacing.

Pin the right side of the fusible interfacing (the smooth side without resin or adhesive) to the right side of the facing. Pin only the edge that needs to be finished (usually the unnotched edge). Sew with a ¼-in. seam allowance. Clip the curves.

Pin the shaped facing to the neck seam with right sides together.

From the right side, press the seam allowance toward the interfacing (**1**). Fold the interfacing to the wrong side along the seamline. Fuse along the fold using the tip of the iron (**2**). Steam-baste the interfacing in place. Trim the interfacing if it goes past the edges or past the front fold. Finish fusing using a press cloth (**3**).

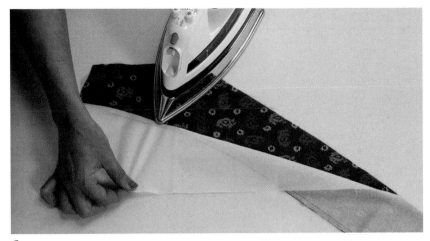

1 *On the right side, press and fuse the seam allowance toward the interfacing.*

Bias Facings

For a designer touch, finish the raw edges of necklines and armholes using a narrow bias binding turned to the inside of the garment; only the topstitching will show. This lightweight treatment is especially appropriate for sheer fabrics and pastel colors that are somewhat sheer.

Cut bias strips as explained in the sidebar on p. 40. Use a ¼-in. seam allowance to join the strips together, making sure the ends of the seamline line up at the sewing line for an even edge. Press the seams open.

Prepare the blouse edge using a ¼-in. seam allowance. Staystitch the neckline or armhole edge. If the pattern has a ⅝-in. seam allowance, staystitch ⅜ in. from the edge and trim next to the staystitching to leave a ¼-in. seam allowance.

To prepare the binding, cut the strip 1½-in. wide on the true bias and 4 in. longer than the edge being finished. Fold the strip in half with wrong sides together, and press lightly with a dry iron. Press the binding to conform to

2 *Tack the interfacing in position to the wrong side of the fabric.*

3 *Fuse the interfacing to the fabric from the wrong side using a press cloth.*

the shape of the neckline, aligning the cut edges to the pattern edge (**1**, p. 66).

Pin the binding to the right side of the garment, keeping the raw edges even. Place pins perpendicular to the seam with the heads extending past the edge. If using in-the-round construction, start pinning at a shoulder seam for the neckline (and at the underarm seam for the armholes). Overlap

Add piping to faced edges or to seams to add color or texture and play up the flattering lines in a blouse.

1 *Press the folded bias strip to conform to the shape of the neckline.*

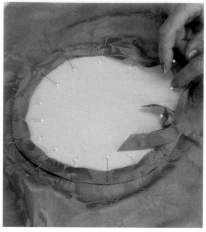

2 *Pin the binding to the right side of the garment, with the raw edges even.*

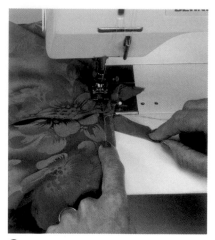

3 *Sew with the garment side up and next to the staystitch line.*

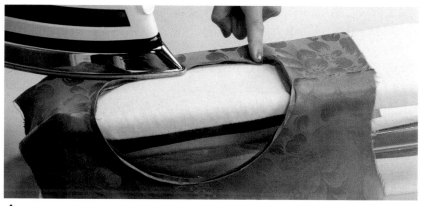

4 *Press the seam allowances toward the binding.*

the ends of the binding and curve them off the cut edge of the seamline **(2)**.

Sew with the garment side up and next to the staystitch line. Use the needle down position, if it's an option on your machine. Stop frequently to adjust the bias edges so that they stay aligned to the neckline edge **(3)**. Clip the seams, and then press the seam allowances toward the bias binding **(4)**.

Fold the binding to the wrong side and press. Topstitch using a ¹/₄-in. seam allowance or edgestitch.

Knit Ribbing

For an interesting detail, forget the facings and sleeve hems and use knit ribbing as an accent and edge finish. Adding ribbed trim to woven fabrics is a contemporary fashion look. Purchase ribbing for the neck and edge trim by the yard.

To maintain the same neckline on the finished blouse, cut away 1 in. to lower it. Measure the neck opening, not including seam allowances.

Cut the ribbing 3 in. wide and three-quarters the length of the neckline opening plus ¹/₂ in. For a 24-in. neckline, $24 \times {}^3/_4 = 18 + {}^1/_2$ in.; cut 18¹/₂ in. by 3 in.

Sew the ends of the ribbing together along its width to form a circle. Use a ¹/₄-in. seam allowance. Finger-press the seam open. With wrong sides together, fold the ribbing in half lengthwise and machine-baste together close to the cut edges. Allow the ribbing to stretch as you baste **(1)**.

To prepare to attach the ribbing, divide the ribbing and neck edge into fourths and mark with a marker or pins. It's more accurate to divide the ribbing into fourths if you stretch it. Note that the shoulder seams are not the midpoints between the center front and center back, unless the blouse has the same neckline front and back.

Pin the basted edge of the ribbing to the right side of the neck seam, matching marks **(2)**. Place the ribbing seam at the center back. Pin between the marks, stretching the ribbing to fit the neckline.

Stitch the neckline with a $\frac{1}{2}$-in. seam allowance **(3)**. Serge the seam or double-stitch and trim the seam to $\frac{1}{4}$ in. Finger-press the neck seam toward the blouse and topstitch the seam at $\frac{1}{8}$ in. **(4)**.

To finish a blouson waist or long sleeve, cut the ribbing 6 in. wide. Cut the length three-quarters the length of the seam or the size of the waist, hip, or wrist measurement plus $\frac{1}{2}$ in. Be sure that the ribbing can stretch to the size of the blouse edge. If it can't, cut the ribbing longer or gather the blouse edge to fit.

1 *Fold the ribbing in half lengthwise and machine-baste the edges.*

2 *Pin the basted edge of the ribbing to the right side of the neck seam.*

3 *Stitch the neckline with a $\frac{1}{2}$-in. seam allowance.*

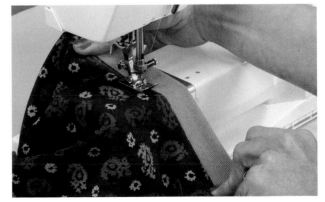

4 *Topstitch the neck seam at $\frac{1}{8}$ in. on the right side.*

Sewing Collars

Beautifully sewn collars have uniform front points or curves and roll smoothly around the neck. Interface the top collar and be sure to position the collar exactly between the end marks along the neckline for professional results.

Curve the upper collar around the undercollar and pin.

Preparing the Collar

Pin the upper collar to the undercollar along the outer seamline, leaving the neck seam open. The neck seam is usually notched. The upper collar is slightly larger than the undercollar, so force the cut edges together. Curve the upper collar around the lower collar and your hand to pin. This distributes the ease.

Points An easy way to make both corners of the collar the same is to sew off the edges at the corners and then resew the corners only by using a short stitch and pivoting at each point. Sewing with seams crossing at the corners gives you even points, and the continuous stitch around the corner prevents the stitches from opening when you trim the seams.

Sew with the undercollar on top. Start sewing the outer seamline at the center back and sew completely off the edge at the point. Repeat for the other half, starting at the center again and overlapping the stitches instead of backstitching to start. Sew both end seams, with seams crossing at the point (**1**).

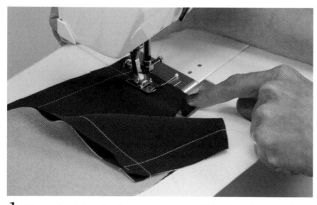

1 *To make identical corners, sew off both edges with the seams crossing.*

2 *Trim and grade the seams and trim the collar points.*

Reinforce each point by shortening the stitch length to 1.5 and sewing a continuous stitch, pivoting at each point. Start the stitching 1 in. from the point, pivot, sew two stitches across, pivot again, and sew for 1 in. Grade the seams and trim the collar points diagonally (**2**).

From the wrong side, press the seam allowances toward the undercollar on a point presser (**3**).

Turn to the right side, using a point turner to push out the point (**4**). Use a long pin to adjust or pull out the point, but be careful not to grab just a few threads of fabric to avoid fraying the corner (**5**).

Finish by pressing the collar, rolling the seam to the under-collar (**6**).

3 *Press the seam allowances toward the undercollar on a point presser.*

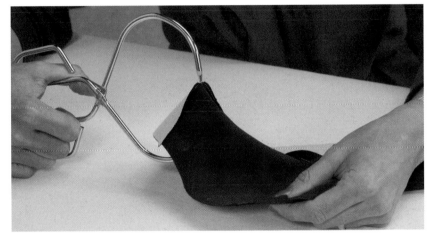

4 *Use a point turner to push out the point.*

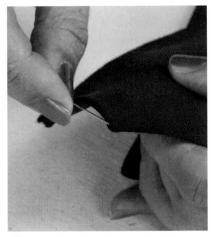

5 *Use a long pin to adjust the point.*

6 *Press the collar, rolling the seam to the undercollar.*

Curves To make sure front edges that curve are the same on both sides, mark the seamline at the front curves only (**1**).

Sew the outer seamline in two steps, starting at the center back. Lift the presser foot often to shape the curve, and apply pressure behind the foot to control stretching (**2**). Trim and notch the curve or pink the seam allowance (**3**).

Press the seam allowances toward the undercollar, but avoid pressing the curves. Understitch the lower collar, being sure to pull the fabric away from the seam to the left and right of the needle. Turn right side out and press, rolling the seam to the undercollar.

1 *Mark the seamline carefully at the front curves.*

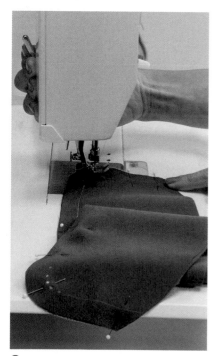

2 *Sewing from the center back, lift the presser foot to control the curve.*

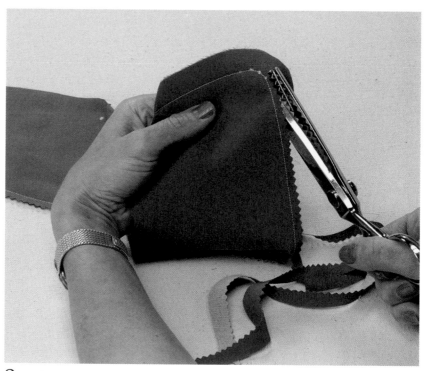

3 *Pink the seam allowance to ensure a smooth curve.*

Collars without a Back Facing

On blouses with front closures, it is very common to have front facings but no back neck facing. There are many variations. The collar can be any shape and size, and the blouse fronts may button or wrap and tie. Use the following directions instead of the pattern directions to attach the collar and you will get a neater neck seam and a smoother transition from the front facing to the back neck seam.

Preparing the Collar

Reinforce-stitch the neck edge of the interfaced upper collar, going 1 in. beyond the shoulder marks. Clip the collar seam allowance to the staystitch at the shoulder marks. Press the seam allowance to the wrong side between the clips (1).

Sew the upper collar to the under-collar, leaving the neck seam open. Trim, press, turn, and press again. Topstitch if your pattern calls for it. Baste the raw edges together at both ends of the collar, stopping ½ in. before the shoulder marks.

Preparing the Neckline
Apply interfacing to the front facings, using the faced-facing technique discussed on pp. 64-65. Press the facing seam allowances under at the shoulder seams. Press the blouse shoulder seams toward the front. Staystitch the blouse and the facing neck seams. Clip the seam allowance to the stay-stitching at ½-in. intervals.

Attaching the Collar
With right sides together, pin the under-collar only to the back neck seam between the shoulder marks. Sew the back neck seam, going ½ in. beyond the shoulder marks (2).

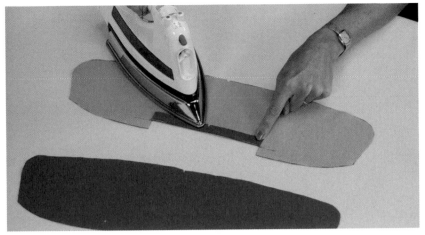

1 *To prepare the collar, reinforce-stitch the neck edge, clip to the staystitch, and press the seam allowance between the clips.*

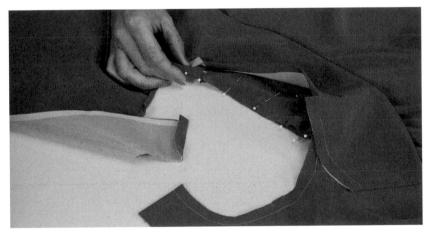

2 *Pin and sew the undercollar to the back neck seam, going ½ in. beyond the shoulder marks.*

3 *Pin and baste the upper collar and undercollar to the front neck seam.*

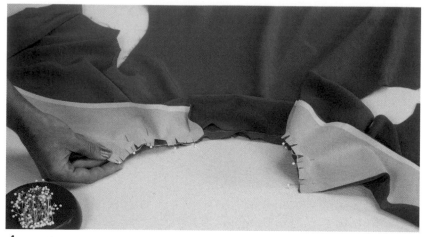

4 *Pin the front facing over the collar from the front fold to the shoulder marks.*

Pin the upper collar and undercollar to the front neck seam, carefully matching markings. Baste from the large dot (end mark) to the shoulder seam at both ends (**3,** p. 71). Make sure the front ends do not move away from the end marks.

Position the front facings over the collar and pin the neck seam from the front fold to the shoulder marks at both ends. Sew with the garment side up, starting at the front fold and stopping at the shoulder marks (**4**).

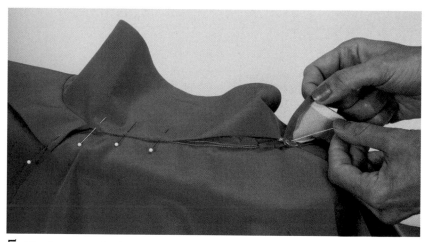

5 *Pin the pressed edge of the upper collar over the neck seam, and then edgestitch.*

Check the collar points and neck seam from the right side. Are the collar points the same length? Are there any tucks in the neck seam? Grade the seam, making additional clips if necessary, and then turn the facings right side out.

Clip the neck seam to the stitchline at the end of the facings. Press the seam toward the collar between the clips. Trim the pressed seam allowance of the upper collar to ³⁄₈ in. and pin the pressed edge of the upper collar over the neck seam. Edgestitch the undercollar between the shoulder seams to secure, or sew by hand with a slipstitch (**5**).

Machine-stitch or slipstitch the folded facing edge to the shoulder seam (**6**).

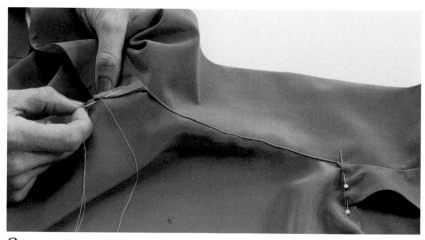

6 *Slipstitch the folded facing edge to the shoulder seam.*

Knitted Collars

Here's another collar idea from ready-to-wear that looks great on camp shirts for men, women, or children and saves sewing time. The best application for knitted collars is as a contrasting or complementary color. It's easier to attach knitted collars using a ¼-in. seam allowance. If your pattern has a ⅝-in. seam allowance, staystitch the neck seam and reduce the seam allowance to ¼ in.

Attaching the Collar Begin by cutting a bias strip 1½ in. wide and long enough to go ¾ in. past the front facings or plackets. Press in half lengthwise. Fold the collar in half crosswise to mark the center back.

Pin the unfinished edge of the collar to the outside neckline, matching end marks and center back (**1**). If necessary, stretch the collar edge to fit the neckline between the marks. Baste the collar to the blouse.

Fold the front facings along the foldline over the front collar with right sides together. Pin and sew the facings in place at the neck seam. Check the length of the collar points and neck seam from the right side.

Pin the bias binding over the collar at the back neck seam, aligning the raw edges. The ends must extend past the facings for a clean finish. Stitch over the neck seam to hold in place (**2**). Clip the seam allowance. Press the binding and seam allowance toward the blouse and pin. Finish by topstitching ¼ in. away from the neck seam, going ½ in. beyond the facing or placket edges at each end (**3**).

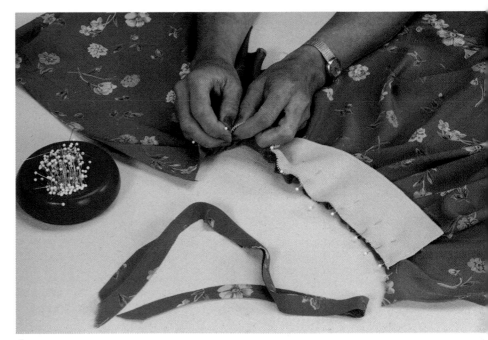

1 *Pin the knit collar to the neckline.*

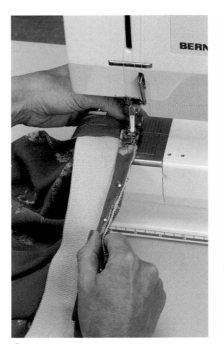

2 *Pin the bias binding over the collar and stitch to hold in place.*

3 *Fold and pin the seam allowance toward the blouse, and then topstitch.*

Collars with a Stand

A collar with a stand is the traditional collar for both men's and ladies' shirts. Lots of seams come together in close proximity, so it's very important to trim seams. This method works best for a smooth band that does not pucker the front edge.

Preparing the Collar Interface the upper collar and collar stand. Sew the collar, trim, press, turn, and press again. Baste the raw edges together using a ¼-in. seam allowance. Topstitch if applicable.

Staystitch the lower edge of the collar stand and press the seam allowance back next to the staystitching. If your blouse has a hidden closure, sew it to the

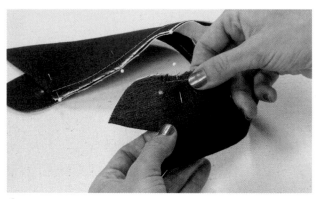

1 *Pin the collar to the collar stand between the marks.*

2 *Pin the stand facing to the right side of the collar and stand, and sew from the center out.*

3 *Trim curves with pinking shears.*

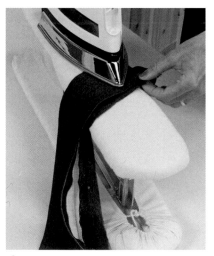

4 *Turn the collar right side out and press.*

5 *Pin the right side of the stand facing to the wrong side of the neckline.*

blouse front before attaching the collar.

Attaching the Collar Pin the finished collar to the collar stand between the collar marks so that the right side of the undercollar faces the right side of the collar stand (**1**). Sew at the machine.

Pin the right side of the stand facing to the right side of the collar and stand. Unfold the collar-stand seam allowance before sewing. Sew with the stand facing on top and from the center out. Stitch ¼ in. past the staystitching (**2**). Compare both ends of the collar and stand from the right side, to make sure they are identical. Trim the seams. Trim curves using pinking shears or cut out notches (**3**). Turn right side out and press the seam (**4**).

Staystitch and clip the blouse neckline. Pin the right side of the stand facing to the wrong side of the neckline and sew (**5**). Turn right side out to be sure the stand encloses the front edge without straining. Trim the seam allowance to ¼ in. and press toward the collar stand.

On the outside, be sure the folded edge covers the neck seam. Adjust if necessary. Trim the seam allowance to ⅜ in. (**6**).

Use double-stick tape or fusible web to hold the fold covering the neck seam in place (**7**). Edgestitch around the entire stand on the right side, starting at a hidden area under the collar (**8**).

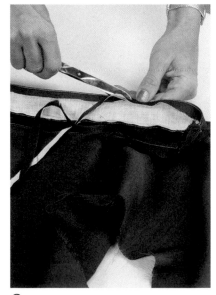

6 *Trim the stand seam allowance to ⅜ in.*

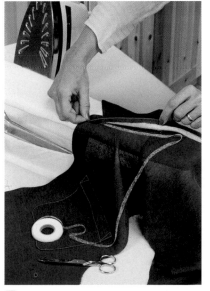

7 *Use fusible web or double-stick tape to hold the stand in place over the neck seam.*

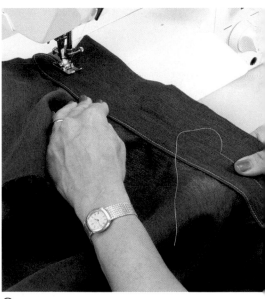

8 *Edgestitch around the stand on the right side.*

Sewing a Yoked Blouse

Shoulder yokes are traditional to classic men's and ladies' shirts. You'll also find them on more feminine blouse styles, designer blouses, shirtwaist dresses, and unlined sporty jackets.

The standard yoke is cut with the lengthwise grain going across the back for stability. For a directional fabric or print, use the cross grain instead.

Most yokes are fully lined or faced so the seams are enclosed and neat. Usually you cut two yokes from the fashion fabric and use one as the facing. If you sew on a printed fabric that has a light background color, the facing print will show through to the outside. To avoid this, cut the facing from a solid-color cotton broadcloth, or another solid fabric, with the same hand and fiber content as the outside fabric. Also use a different facing fabric when the outside fabric is too bulky.

The two applications presented here facilitate sewing the yoke. Sewing is done entirely by machine, just as in ready-to-wear, and topstitching is optional. The results are professional and durable. The yoke application you select depends on the type of collar the blouse has.

On the standard shirt application, the collar goes on *after* the yoke is in place and encloses the neck seam. Use this yoke application for collars with a stand and all fashion collars that go to or extend past the front edge of the neckline.

On the blouse-type application, the collar must be attached to the neck seam between the two marks before attaching the front facing and yoke facing as a unit. Use this yoke application when the collar stops a distance in from the front edge of the neckline. An example of this type of collar is the notched collar.

Check your pattern guidesheet to see which collar application you have and follow the appropriate method.

Mark the yoke and yoke facing using snips instead of fabric marker. Snips identify marks easily on both the right and wrong side of the fabric. The snips will be important later when the yoke is completed and you attach the collar and sleeves. Be sure to snip the center back, shoulders, and any dots and notches.

Standard Shirt Yoke

Sew the yoke to the shirt front and back with right sides together (**1**). If you're adding shoulder pads, attach Velcro-brand fasteners to the yoke facing (see the sidebar on p. 79).

1 *To prepare, sew the yoke to the shirt front and back with right sides together.*

2 *With the right side up, roll the shirt front and back into position over the yoke.*

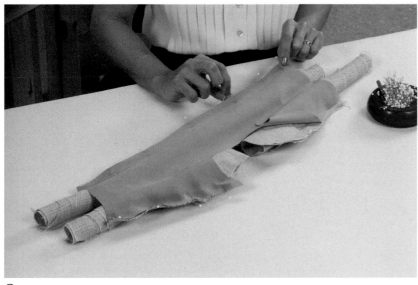

3 *With right sides together, pin the yoke facing over the rolls at the shoulder seams and back yoke seam.*

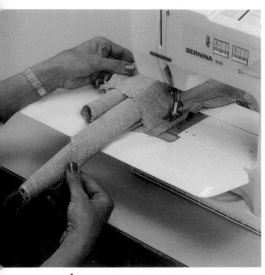

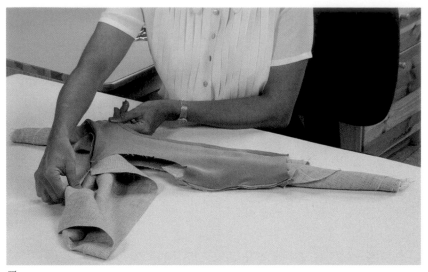

4 *Sew the yoke and shoulder seams again over the previous stitching.*

5 *Turn the shirt right side out by pulling it through the neck opening.*

6 *Press the yoke.*

Place the shirt flat on a table with the right side up. Roll the shirt back and shirt fronts into position over the yoke (**2,** p. 77).

Pin the yoke facing over the rolled blouse at the shoulder seams and back yoke seam with right sides together (**3,** p. 77). (The yoke and facing are right sides together; the blouse fronts and back are sandwiched between.) Sew the seams again with the yoke facing up over the previous stitching (**4**). Trim or grade the seams.

Turn the shirt right side out through the neck opening (**5**). Press the yoke (**6**). Staystitch the neck edge, and you are ready to attach the collar.

REMOVABLE SHOULDER PADS

It makes a lot of sense to use removable shoulder pads in blouses. For one thing, depending on how the blouse is worn, the pads may not always be necessary. For another, removable pads are easier to wash—even washable pads tend to clump into a shape that defies description after washing.

For ease of removal, I use a Velcro-brand strip to attach the pads to the blouse shoulder seam. For a standard shoulder seam, position a 2-in.-long strip on top of the seam allowance. The nappy side faces the body when you wear the blouse. Stitch the strip to the seam allowance only.

For a blouse with a yoke, attach the strip to the right side of the yoke facing along the shoulder line. The shoulder line lies between the shoulder mark at the neck seam and the sleeve dot at the armhole seam. Stitch around the strip.

If you prefer permanently attached shoulder pads, on blouses with kimono sleeves or drop-shoulder set-in sleeves sew raglan-style shoulder pads to the shoulder-seam allowance using a catchstitch or backstitch. Stop sewing where the shoulder curve starts. On yoked blouses, sew to the yoke facing only. Sew regular shoulder pads with the widest edge extending $\frac{1}{2}$ in. into the sleeve cap.

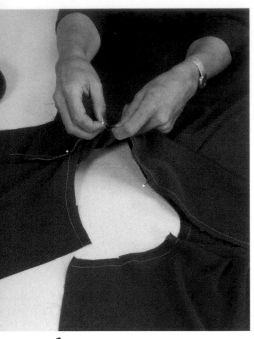

1 *Pin the collar to the neckline with the undercollar facing the right side.*

2 *Trim the facing shoulder seams to ¼ in. near the neckline for a distance of 1 in.*

3 *Pin the right side of the facing unit to the right side of the blouse at the neck edge and sew.*

Blouse-Type Yoke

Use this method anytime the front facings and yoke enclose the collar, as on a notched collar.

Sew the yoke to the blouse front and back with right sides together. Trim the shoulder seams to ⅜ in. near the neckline only for a distance of 1 in. Press the trimmed section toward the yoke.

Staystitch the neck edge. Baste the raw edges of the collar together ⅜ in. in from the edge. Pin the collar to the neckline, matching symbols, with the undercollar facing the right side of the neckline (1). Clip the neck edge where necessary. Machine-baste.

Stitch the yoke facing to the blouse front facings at the shoulders. Trim the shoulder seams to ¼ in. near the neckline

4 *Clip facings where necessary and sew the neck seam.*

5 *Check that the collar points are the same length.*

only for a distance of 1 in. **(2)**. Press the trimmed section toward the yoke. Staystitch the neck edge on the front facing and the yoke facing unit.

Pin the right side of the facing unit to the right side of the blouse at the neck edge, matching symbols **(3)**. Clip facings where necessary and sew the neck seam **(4)**. Sew the front edges, and then grade and clip the seams. Before grading and clipping the neck seam, check that both collar points are the same length and an equal distance from the front fold or seam **(5)**. Press the neck seam and front edges.

At the front shoulder seams, pin the yoke to the yoke facing with right sides together **(6)**. (The blouse front is sandwiched between the two.) Place pins along the stitchline and turn right side out before sewing to check

6 *At the front shoulder, pin the yoke to the yoke facing, placing pins along the stitchline.*

Sewing a Yoked Blouse   **81**

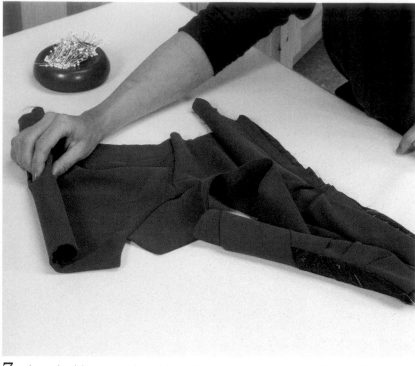

the placement. Sew the shoulder seams again between the collar and the armhole over the previous stitching. You will not be able to sew completely to the collar—just sew as far as possible without distorting the seam. Trim or grade the shoulder seams.

Place the blouse flat on a table with the right side up. Roll the shirt back and shirt fronts into position over the yoke (7). Wrap the yoke facing over the rolled blouse, and match the back facing seam to the sewn back yoke seam (8). (The yoke and facing are right sides together; blouse fronts and back are sandwiched between.)

Sew the back yoke seam again (9). This time pull the blouse to the right side through a shoulder opening (10).

7 *Place the blouse on the table right side up and roll the shirt back and fronts into position over the yoke.*

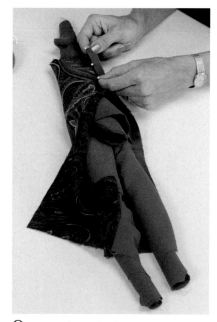

8 *Wrap the yoke facing over the rolled blouse and pin.*

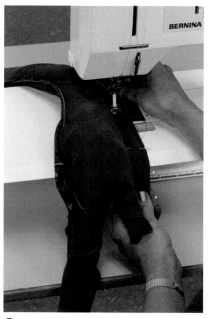

9 *Sew the back yoke seam again over the previous stitching.*

10 *Pull the blouse to the right side through a shoulder opening.*

Sewing the Sleeves

Blouses are designed with a variety of sleeve styles. The set-in sleeve is the most widely used application, and it has many variations.

Set-in sleeves on shirts and blouses with extended or dropped shoulders have a flat sleeve cap with a minimum amount of ease. Attach this type of set-in sleeve using the flat method.

Other types of set-in sleeves have a rounded cap that can be slightly rounded but smooth, full and gathered or pleated. The rounded cap always measures more than the armhole and needs easestitching, gathers, or pleats to control the fullness before the sleeve is set into the armscye. Form pleats along the sleeve cap the same way you form pleats along the shoulder or sleeve bottom, being sure to align the cut edges as well as the foldlines. Sleeves with any of these sleeve-cap variations must be set into the armhole with in-the-round construction, after you sew the shoulder seams and side seams of the blouse and the underarm seam of the sleeve.

Raglan sleeves are joined to the blouse by a diagonal seam between the neckline and the underarm. Kimono and dolman sleeves are an extension of the blouse front and back. Sew these sleeves as you would sew any other seam, matching the appropriate notches.

Flat-Sleeve Construction

Flat-sleeve construction is the easiest and allows for adjustment to the blouse and sleeve width after the sleeve is set in without complications. Follow these steps to prevent tucks or puckers along the sleeve cap.

Position the sleeve to match the body of the blouse (**1**). Pin the sleeve to the armhole with right sides together. Pin the center mark, notches, and ends. Place

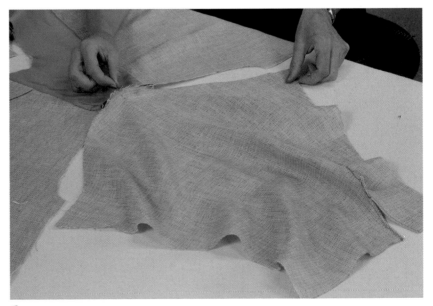

1 *Position and pin the sleeve to the body of the blouse.*

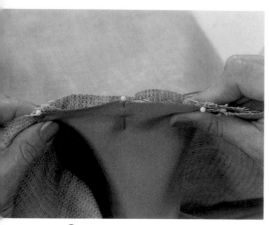

2 *Pin the sleeve to the body, squeezing the seamline to check that ease is distributed evenly.*

pins perpendicular to the edge. Use lots of pins to force the edges together and distribute ease evenly.

To head off trouble, check ease distribution. Squeeze the armhole seam between your fingers along the sewing line. If you can flatten the ease, you've done a good job **(2)**. If you feel a fold when you squeeze the seam, unpin and redistribute the ease in that area.

Sew with the garment up and the sleeve down, stopping frequently to check the lower layer as you go **(3)**.

For an even stitch around curves, sew the first row following the right side of the presser foot to the edge of the sleeve cap. Sew the second row following the right side of the foot to the first stitch. These stitches may not be exactly $3/8$ in. and $5/8$ in. on your machine, but they are close enough. The curve will be easier to follow and the stitchline will be smooth.

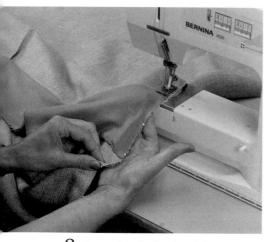

3 *Sew with the body of the garment on top, checking frequently to ensure that the sleeve is smooth.*

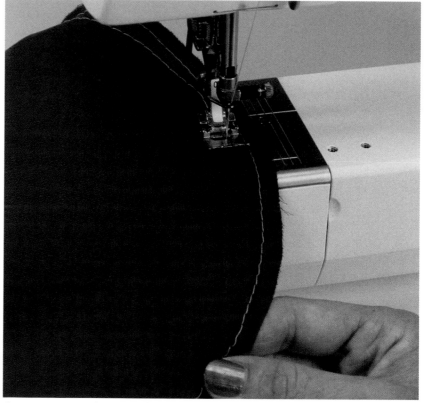

Sew two rows of easestitch around the cap of the sleeve to ease in fullness.

Round-Sleeve Construction

The sleeve that requires in-the-round construction has a controlled shape and more ease in the cap. The standard way to ease the sleeve cap is to use two rows of easestitch along the cap, as shown in the photo at right on the facing page. Baste at ⅜ in. and at ⅝ in. (the same as for gathers, see p. 63).

Here are two alternative ways to ease the cap that are quicker and neater than the standard method and avoid easestitching:

Ease in the cap using a large stitch (eight or fewer stitches per inch). Hold the fabric to the left and right of the foot. Then pull away from the foot with both hands as you force extra fabric under the foot by pushing the fabric back as you sew (see the top photo at right).

Alternatively, use 1¼-in. bias tricot (such as Seams Great) to ease in the cap. Sew the tricot to the wrong side of the sleeve cap with a basting stitch. Stretch the tricot as you sew using a ½-in. seam allowance (see the bottom photo at right).

When easing in the cap with a large stitch, pull the fabric away from the stitch on both sides of the foot as you sew.

When easing in the cap with bias tricot, pull on the bias strip and force extra fabric under the foot as you sew.

Whichever method you use to ease the sleeve cap, sew in the sleeve as follows:

Pin the sleeve cap to the armhole with right sides together (1).

Match side seams, notches, and other match points. Distribute ease evenly along the cap. Starting near the underarm seam, with the blouse side up, stitch the armhole seam (2).

1 *Pin the cap to the armhole with right sides together, distributing ease evenly.*

2 *With the blouse side up, stitch the armhole seam, checking that the sleeve is smooth.*

BIAS-TRICOT BOUND SEAM

For a clean finish after the sleeve is set in, use 1¼-in.-wide bias tricot to bind and finish the armhole. Pull the tricot lengthwise to see which way it curls. Starting at the underarm, center the tricot binding over the seamline so that it curls away from the blouse, and then straight-stitch the seam (1). Trim the seam allowance to ¼ in. Finger-press the binding up and around the seam allowances, and then stitch in the seam allowance with a narrow zigzag stitch (2).

Note that ⅝-in. bias-tricot binding can be used for a clean finish on shaped facings (see p. 64).

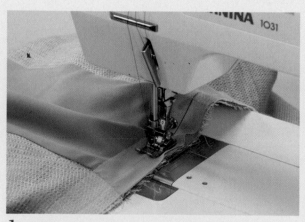

1 *Center a strip of bias-tricot binding over the seamline and sew.*

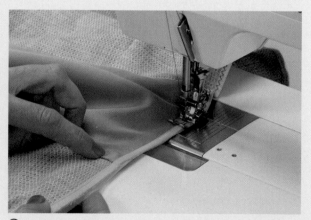

2 *Fold the binding over the seam allowance and sew with a zigzag stitch.*

Plackets

Finish sleeves with a continuous-lap placket or with a simplified sleeve opening with the binding eliminated.

Continuous-Lap Sleeve Placket

The continuous-lap placket is a versatile technique that has many applications. On a blouse, a lengthwise strip of self-fabric is used to bind the opening of the sleeve, but this placket is also found on skirts, children's clothing, overalls, jumpers, and neck openings on T-shirts.

Whenever possible, cut the placket bindings along the selvage. Use the pattern or cut a strip 1 1/4 in. wide and twice the length of the marked opening along the stitch-line. Fold and press under 1/4 in. on one long side.

On the sleeve, mark the sewing line on the wrong side. Reinforce-stitch on the stitchline, taking two stitches across the dart point. Cut the center of the dart to the point, making sure to cut to but not through the stitched point (**1,** p. 88).

Pin the right side of the binding to the right side of the placket opening. (Pin the reinforced stitching line to the binding sewing line 1/4 in. in from the edge.) Mark the center of the placket with a pin (**2,** p. 88).

1 *Reinforce the stitchline of the placket and cut through the center to the point.*

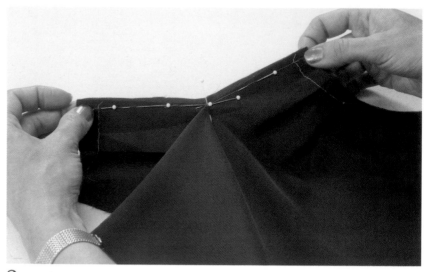

2 *Pin the right side of the binding to the right side of the placket, marking the center with a pin.*

When sewing a continuous-lap placket, the point is the critical area. Lift the presser foot with the needle in the down position to make sure you are pivoting exactly at the point. You can walk the machine manually over the center pin so the fabric won't shift.

3 *Stitch a ¹/₄-in. seam along the binding edge, pivoting the sleeve fabric away from the needle at the center.*

Stitch a ¹/₄-in. seam to the point, where the stitches are very close to the sleeve edge but remain ¹/₄ in. from the binding edge. The stitch should be directly on top of, or a hairline in from, the reinforce stitching (3).

At the point, leave the needle in the fabric, raise the presser foot, and pivot the sleeve fabric away from the needle. Straighten the sewing line and sew to the edge.

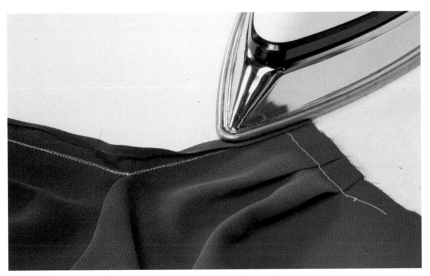

4 *Enclose the raw edge with the folded edge and press.*

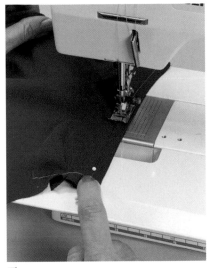

5 *Edgestitch the placket edge from the right side.*

6 *Turn and press the front placket edge to the inside.*

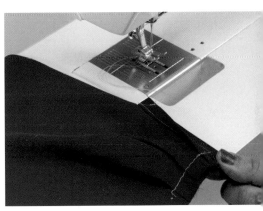

7 *Stitch diagonally across the upper edge of the placket fold.*

Press the stitchline flat, and then press the seam allowances toward the opening. Bring the folded edge over the stitchline, enclosing the raw edge, and press (**4**).

Edgestitch the placket binding from the right side. To do this, pin along the seamline on the right side and be sure to catch the folded edge on the bottom (**5**).

Turn and press the front placket to the inside, and then baste the lower edge in place (**6**). On the inside, stitch the placket fold diagonally (**7**).

Simplified Sleeve Opening

This simplified sleeve opening is used by Vogue/Butterick. The opening edges are turned under and edgestitched, thereby eliminating the binding.

This sleeve opening works well on all fabrics but is especially good for sheer fabrics. Use the following directions and sewing sequence instead of the pattern and you'll have more control of the fabric and achieve a neat miter near the dart.

Mark the dart sewing line and any dots on the wrong side. Slash along the line to the mark (**1**). Turn the opening edges to the inside along the foldlines (3/8 in.) and press. Turn under the raw edges to the foldline, tapering to nothing at the point, and press (**2, 3**).

Edgestitch the folded edges as far as possible, making sure to go 1 in. past the dot. Pull the thread tails to help you get started (**4**).

Stitch the dart from the dot, on the foldline to the point. Make sure that the folded edges are aligned, and that you start sewing exactly on the edge (**5**). Be sure to lock in the stitch at both ends.

1 *Slash along the dart centerline to the mark.*

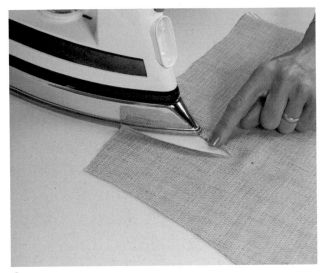

2 *Turn under and press the raw edges, tapering to nothing at the point.*

3 *For greater control, use a pin to tuck under the narrow edges.*

4 *Edgestitch the folded edges using the tail of the thread to get started.*

5 *Stitch from the dot to the point, making sure that the folded edges are aligned.*

Sewing Cuffs

Sew-on cuffs enclose the lower edge of the sleeve, which may be gathered, pleated, or simply tapered at the bottom. Use the following sequence to eliminate the problem of catching the underside of the cuff while sewing from the top.

Standard Cuff

To prepare the cuffs, mark dots and any other symbols on the wrong side of the notched edge only. Snip the foldlines. Fuse interfacing to the unnotched half, and press under a scant $5/8$-in. seam allowance on the unnotched edge **(1)**. The notched half of the cuff is the cuff facing and the unnotched half is the outside cuff.

If your fabric stretches easily, stabilize the edge you are pressing by staystitching $1/2$ in. away from the edge. Then press the seam allowance so that the stitchline is turned slightly to the back.

Fold the cuff right sides together along the foldline. Stitch the ends, opening out the folded seam allowance. Trim, press, turn right sides out, and then press the seams and the foldline **(2)**.

Pin the right side of the cuff facing to the wrong side of the sleeve, matching symbols. Stitch the seam **(3)**.

Press the seam toward the cuff facing and trim **(4)**. Press and then pin the folded edge so that it covers the seamline **(5)**. To finish, edgestitch the cuff, keeping the fabric taut **(6)**.

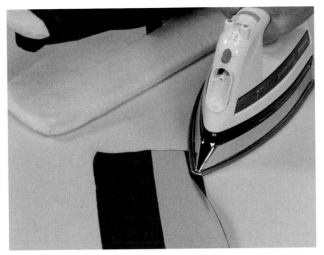

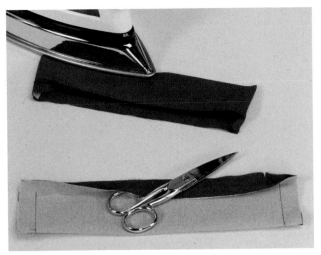

1 *Prepare the cuff by fusing the interfacing and pressing a ⅝-in. seam allowance on the unnotched half.*

2 *Stitch the ends of the cuff, and then turn right sides out to press the seams and the foldline.*

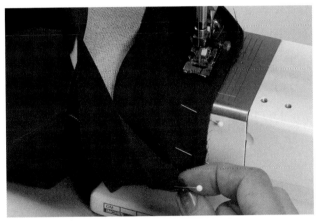

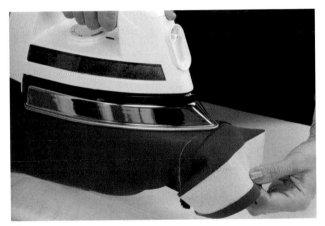

3 *Pin the right side of the cuff facing to the wrong side of the sleeve and stitch the seam.*

4 *Press the seam toward the cuff facing.*

5 *Press the folded edge so that it covers the seamline.*

6 *Edgestitch from the right side, keeping the fabric taut.*

No-Cuff Cuff

Here's a cuff variation with a
lapped opening that eliminates
the cuff pattern. Instead of sewing
on a separate cuff, extend the
bottom marks of the sleeve to the
new longer length (see p. 36).
Also lengthen the placket binding
by the same amount. This sleeve
has a slender tapered bottom and
an elongated hidden placket that
works nicely with tiny buttons
and buttonholes or with buttons
and loops.

To begin, reinforce-stitch the
placket opening (but don't cut the
center yet). Form pleats by pinning
the two sewing lines right sides
together and stitching on the
marked lines. Be sure to backstitch at both ends. Press the
pleats toward the opening.

Close and finish the blouse and
sleeve side seams. (If the sleeve
gets sewn into the blouse flat, you
can sew just the lower 6 in. of the
sleeve side seam.) Staystitch the
lower edge 1/4 in. away from the
bottom. Press up the hem 1/4 in.,
then 3/8 in. Cut the center of the
dart to the point. Be sure to cut to
but not through the stitched point.
Topstitch the hem 1/4 in. from the
edge, starting and ending at the
center of the placket opening.

If you are using button loops (see
the sidebar on pp. 96-97), attach
them now, on the right side of the
front sleeve opening, matching
the sewing lines. Use double-
sided tape to hold the loops in

place. The loops should be facing away from the center of the dart.

Pin the right side of the placket to the right side of the placket opening. (Pin the reinforced stitching line to the binding sewing line 1/4 in. in from the edge.) Make sure you have a 5/8-in. seam allowance extending past the hem at both ends of the placket.

Stitch a 1/4-in. seam to the point, where the stitches are very close to the sleeve edge but remain 1/4 in. in from the binding edge. The stitch should also be placed a hairline in from the reinforce stitching. At the point, leave the needle in the fabric, raise the presser foot, and pivot the sleeve fabric away from the needle. Straighten the sewing line and sew to the edge, and then press the seam allowances toward the opening.

Fold and pin the placket lengthwise at both ends with right sides together. Bring the folded edge 1/8 in. past the placket seam to cover it. Sew both ends of the placket just next to the hemline. Turn the corners out to check the hem alignment. Trim the seam allowance to 1/4 in. Turn right side out and press the folded edge to cover the seamline. Pin from the right side and topstitch on the placket 1/16 in. away from the seam. Instead of backstitching at both ends, taper the stitch length to zero. You will need to use the thread tails to pull the fabric back at the beginning.

Turn and press the front placket to the inside and slipstitch the lower placket edge to the hem edge. On the inside, stitch the placket fold diagonally.

Position, pin, and sew the placket to the blouse.

SEWING BUTTON LOOPS

Button loops are fabric closures used on cuffs, as well as on front and back closings. Begin by making a test loop to check the diameter of the tubing. On blouse-weight fabrics, I try to make the finest tube possible that can be turned using a bobby pin.

Making the Tubing

Start with a ¾-in.-wide bias strip, increasing the width if necessary for your fabric. Fold the bias in half lengthwise with right sides together. Sew halfway between the fold and the cut edges, stretching the bias as you sew (1). Sew again to avoid popped stitches and to true the sewing line. If you pull erratically as you sew, it will be reflected in the width of the tubing.

To turn the tubing right side out, first snip an opening in the fold ½ in. in from one end. Using a bobby pin with smooth tips, insert one tip through the end of the tubing and the other tip through the little opening before it enters the tube (2). Use the bobby pin to slide the tube through to the opening at the other end. (It's easy to turn the tubing right side out when the fabric is silky. If you're sewing with a fabric like linen or cotton that doesn't slide well, use a fabric tube turner like "Miniturn" to help the tubing along.)

Determining the Length of the Loops

To determine the length of tubing for each loop, first draw a vertical line on a sheet of paper ⅝ in. away from the straight edge. This distance represents the seam allowance and the button-placement line. For a placket opening, draw the line ¼ in. away from the straight edge.

Center the button on the button-placement line; you can use tape to hold it in place. Cut a neat straight edge at one end of the tubing. Lay the tubing around the button, starting and ending at the cut edge. Pin or tape the tubing in place.

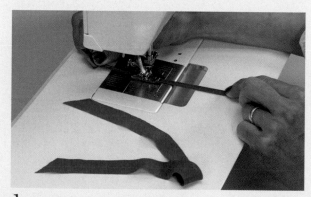

1 Stretch and sew a strip of folded bias tape.

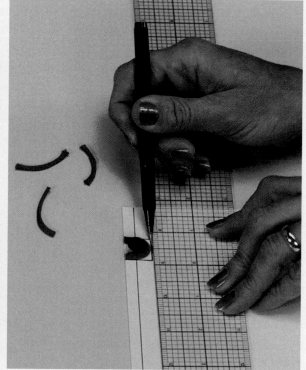

2 Snip one end and insert a bobby pin to turn the tube.

3 Make a sewing guide to determine the length of the loop.

Mark where the tubing crosses the button line above and below the button. This distance is called the spread. Also mark the outermost edge of the loop curve. The width equals the distance from the button-line/seamline to the outer curve. For uniform loops, use these two distances to make a sewing guide (3).

Making a Sewing Guide

You need a narrow strip of paper equal in length or longer than the distance between the top and bottom button. Cash-register paper is a good width, but any crisp paper with a straight edge will do.

If the seam allowance is $5/8$ in., draw a line $5/8$ in. away from the straight edge. To mark the width, draw a line next to the seamline equal to the width at the outer edge of the loops. If the loops go into a continuous-lap placket, use a $1/4$-in. seam allowance.

Draw one line $1/4$ in. away from the straight edge. Mark a line for the loop width, next to the $1/4$ in. line.

To place loops one next to the other, mark the distance of the spread along the sewing line for each button you are using. To space loops apart, mark the spread, then the space, and alternate for the number of buttons you are using.

Use double-sided tape to hold the loops in place. Position the tape next to the sewing line in the seam allowance. Sew the loops to the sewing guide along the sewing line using small stitches (4) and tear away the paper beyond the seam allowance and under the loops.

Attaching the Loops

Peel away the backing paper on the double-sided tape (5). Use the second side of the tape to hold the loops in place on the blouse (6).

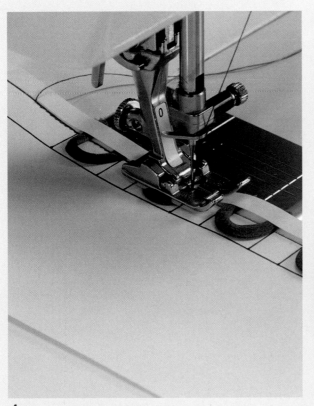

4 Use double-sided tape to hold the loops in place as you sew them to the guide.

5 Peel away the backing paper.

6 Use the other side of the tape to hold the loops in place on the blouse.

Machine-Stitched Hems

The best hem finishes for washable garments are machine stitched. Machine-stitched hems give a sturdy finish that is quick and easy to sew.

The machine-stitched hems discussed in this section reproduce the look of ready-to-wear. They are not just for bottom edges, but can finish collars, too.

Turned and Stitched Hems

For a ⅝-in. hem allowance, press under a ¼-in. hem. Press again ⅜ in. from the first fold. Sew from the right side with a straight stitch, starting at the front edge or at a side seam. Use a seam allowance that is ¼ in. away from the bottom edge.

This same technique can be used on a wide hem, too. Press under half the hem allowance twice and stitch. For a 1-in. hem, press under ½ in. twice and sew about ⅜ in. from the bottom.

On fabrics that have surface texture, a soft drape, or a loose weave (such as crêpe de chine, georgette, rayon challis, and

To press curved edges on shirt-tail hems, stitch ¼ in. from the cut edge, applying pressure behind the presser foot to ease outside curves and stretch inside curves. Press under along the stitch-line and press again ⅜ in. from the first fold. This time, stitch wrong side up and close to the first fold.

1 *Stitch a second line close to the first stitching line.*

handkerchief linen), it's possible to stretch the edge when pressing hems in place. To avoid this problem, use a staystitch to mark and stabilize the first foldline, and then press along the staystitch line. Press the second fold and topstitch.

Use the following option when you want a very narrow hem that is turned under and edgestitched:

Machine-stitch ⅛ in. below the desired length. Press the edge on the stitching line to the wrong side. Stitch a second line close to the fold (1). Trim the seam/hem allowance close to the stitching and press. Turn the hem edge to the wrong side, enclosing the raw edge. Stitch again close to the edge (2).

Serged and Stitched If you have a serger, serge the edge and press under the hem allowance. Sew from the right side. Use a seam allowance ⅛ in. to ¼ in. less than the hem allowance.

Rolled Hems

You can sew a machine-rolled hem on a machine or serger by sewing a satin stitch on the edge of your fabric. I prefer to use the buttonhole foot to do this because the groove at the bottom of the foot is just the right width for the satin or buttonhole stitch and it keeps the edge in place. The machine embroidery foot has a wide groove that makes it harder to control. There is also a universal foot available that lets you position the satin stitch over the edge.

This stitch works beautifully on natural fibers and synthetics that are tightly woven such as crêpe de chine and charmeuse. Always do a test to see if it works on your fabric and to practice sewing on the edge. For smooth, even stitches, try using cotton machine-embroidery thread.

2 *Turn the hem to enclose the raw edge and stitch again.*

Sew a buttonhole stitch over the straight stitch and cut edge (the back side of the stitch is shown).

Trim the hem to the desired finished length. Using the buttonhole foot and setting for the buttonhole stitch, sew along the neatly cut edge of the cloth. If the hem is on the bias or off grain, you'll get a lettuce edge. This ruffled look is caused by the grain stretching as you sew. (You've probably seen this effect on ready-to-wear.) If you don't want a lettuce edge, first sew a straight stitch along the desired length and trim next to the stitch. Sew the buttonhole stitch over the straight stitch and cut edge.

SIDE SLITS

For a different fashion look, you can add side slits or vents to any blouse or top without changing the pattern seams. Slits can be short— 3 in. is a common length—or as long as you want them to be. A tunic-length top can have very long slits. The nice thing about long slits is that you can wear them in different ways. Wear the blouse out and belted one day, and tie the ends of the slits at one side the next for an elegant draped effect (as shown in the photo on p. 106).

If you want to be able to tie the slits, the ends need to be at least 10 in. long. Mark the slit opening 2 in. below where you want to tie it and add to the length of your blouse so that you have 11 in. below the mark at both front and back. This amount includes a narrow hem. For example, to tie at the waist, start the slit 2 in. below the waist and allow 11 in. of material below that point.

Use French seams to sew the side seams, stopping the first row of stitches 1/2 in. above the opening mark. Trim the seam to the end of the stitching only. Sew the second stitch to the opening mark. Clip the seam allowance to the seamline and mark 1/2 in. above the opening.

Sew horizontal hems first, pressing under 1/4 in., then 3/8 in., and stitching the inner fold. Press each slit opening in 1/4 in., then 3/8 in. (as with a hem), and stitch close to the inner fold. Sew from the lower edge, pivot 1/4 in. above the opening, sew across, pivot, and continue down the other side.

Sew the hem and slits from the right side. For a neat start and finish don't backstitch—reduce the stitch length to zero instead. Use the thread tails to pull the fabric back when you start to sew.

Closures

Purchase closures in the trims and notion department. Your pattern lists the type and size you need.

Buttons and buttonholes are functional and can be decorative if you want them to be or hidden if the blouse has a hidden front closure. Other closures such as hooks and eyes and snaps are not meant to be noticed.

Sewing a Hidden Closure

For a different look, add this easy hidden closure to any pattern you already own and like—or substitute this simple method for cutting and sewing a pattern with a hidden closure.

On collars with a stand and other collars that enclose the neck seam from edge to edge, attach the hidden closure prior to attaching the collar. This way the top edge of the placket is also finished by the collar.

Fold the placket in half lengthwise, with right sides together. Sew the bottom and side seams using a ¼-in. seam allowance. Leave the top open, turn right side out, and press. Place the placket behind the right front so that the placket edge is set back ¹⁄₁₆ in. from the blouse front edge. Place the placket hem 1 in. or more above the blouse bottom.

Pin and machine-baste along the edge of the lengthwise placket seam with the longest basting stitch you have (see the top photo on p. 102). If you are sewing on a delicate fabric, avoid pin holes by using double-sided tape or a very

SEWING A DECORATIVE PLACKET

If you opt to add a decorative placket to the outside of the blouse, it needs to have an interesting shape. Use some paper to experiment with different shapes. I like to start out with a large rectangle the size of the outermost dimensions to keep the shape within a maximum usable size range for the blouse front. Then you have lots of options, such as curving corners and drawing in contour or free-form shapes. Keep in mind that the placket will be topstitched to the blouse front. The placket can be used to cover the blouse buttonholes, or it can extend past the front edge and have exposed buttonholes.

Once you've made the pattern, be sure to cut on the lengthwise grain. Cut two plackets with a ¼-in. seam allowance. Sew the placket pieces with right sides together, leaving a small opening at the least conspicuous place in the area that gets stitched to the blouse front. Use this opening to turn the placket right side out.

Clip or notch any curves or corners. Turn to the right side and press. Turn in the seam allowances at the opening and press. Position the placket to the blouse front and edgestitch in place.

Pin the hidden placket in place along the front edge of the blouse.

narrow strip of fusible web to hold the placket in place. For the placket to look centered, the sewing line must be twice the distance between the center front and the finished front edge. If the distance from center front to finished front edge is ³/₄ in., sew 1½ in. in. Mark in the topstitching line, or follow the basting line if it is straight and in the right place. Start the topstitching at the neck seam, pivot at the lower placket edge, and end at the front edge. Tie the threads and use a hand sewing needle to bury them between the layers.

The hidden placket can also be added to a blouse with a notched collar or a V-neckline. Start the placket ½ in. above the top button. End it 1 in. above the bottom hem or just below the bottom button.

To sew plackets whose top edge is not enclosed by the collar, fold the placket in half lengthwise and sew with a ¼-in. seam allowance. Leave a 2-in. opening along the lengthwise seam to turn it right side out.

Buttonhole Placement and Size

Machine-sewn buttonholes are done differently on every sewing machine, but the rules for determining size, marking, and placement are the same. Button-holes go on the right side of the blouse front as you are wearing it. Mark placement when the blouse is completed.

The buttonhole size should equal the diameter of the button plus $1/8$ in. On buttons with irregular shapes, measure the widest point and add $1/8$ in. Test the size—sometimes you can make a smaller buttonhole. If the button has a rounded top, measure the diameter over the curve and add $1/8$ in. For a ball button, measure the circumference by wrapping a narrow strip of paper around the middle and marking the size. Make the buttonhole half this amount plus $1/8$ in.

If you purchase the button size listed on the pattern and the pattern placement marks work for you, use the pattern tissue to mark both placement and size; otherwise, change the size and placement.

The top-button position can't be changed by much. Determine where you want the bottom button. Pin-mark any stress areas such as the bust or waist. You can avoid placing a button under a waistband or belt. Considering these different factors helps you personalize the button placement. Place buttons on all the essential areas, and add additional buttons in between so they look evenly spaced. Measure the space between each and use the median amount. Pin-mark the spacing.

Use vertical buttonholes on placket openings centered on the band. Use horizontal buttonholes on all other openings. Horizontal buttonholes are placed to extend $1/8$ in. beyond the center front toward the edge. Be sure the buttonhole marks are on grain and parallel or at right angles to the front edge.

How you mark buttonholes depends on your sewing machine. On some machines you need to mark the end marks. On others you need to mark only the starting point. Use a delicate hand and keep marking to a minimum. On some fabrics you can use tape to mark the ends.

USING BUTTONS CREATIVELY

The best button choice isn't always the best match for the fabric. To use buttons as a focal point, try the following:

• Use a different button shape or a different button color in each position on the blouse.

• Use different vintage buttons on the same garment.

• Cover blouse buttons with fabric from one skirt or different skirts or bottoms you plan to wear with it. (When using different fabrics together be sure that cleaning does not cause problems such as color running.)

• Sew a separate button placket for reversible vests. Purchase a 1-in.-wide grosgrain ribbon, turn under the cut edges twice, and stitch. Attach buttons according to the buttonhole spacing.

When sewing buttons, each time you insert the needle through the hole to the back, angle the needle so that you keep the stitches close together. This technique prevents the stitches on the back side of the blouse from looking like a road map.

If you sew a button to a single layer of fabric or to fine fabrics that aren't interfaced, you can expect the button to tear a hole in the fabric. Use small circles of felt, like the ones used for button-down collars on men's shirts. If you have the option, place the felt between the facing and the outside; otherwise, place it on the back side of the fabric.

Sewing the Buttons

To determine button placement, pin the blouse closed, overlapping the center fronts or center backs. On horizontal buttonholes, push a pin through the end of each buttonhole that is closest to the front edge and mark the button placement on the left front. On vertical buttonholes, insert the pin ¼ in. from the top edge. Be sure all the dot marks are an equal distance from the edge on the blouse center.

Sew buttons in place using a double strand of thread. For a neater application, start sewing underneath the button and use a few small backstitches instead of a knot.

Sew-Through Buttons Sew-through buttons need a thread shank to allow some room for the buttonhole layer to fit under the button; otherwise, you get puckering around the button. Use a spacer under the button or an object over the button to produce a thread shank when you sew. Bring the needle up through one of the holes. Position a pin or toothpick on top of the button between the holes you are sewing. Take the needle down through the second hole and through the back of the cloth. Repeat five times. If the button has four holes, go through each set three times.

To finish, remove the pin or toothpick, pull the button away from the fabric, and wind the thread around the shank a few times. The longer the shank the more times you wind. If you wind too much, you start to shorten the shank. To secure the ends, backstitch into the fabric at the foot of the shank. Insert the needle between the layers and bring the thread out about 1 in. away to cut the ends.

Shank Buttons Attach shank buttons with short stitches sewn through the shank. You don't need to lengthen the shank for blouse-weight fabrics. The direction of the shank must be aligned with the direction of the buttonhole to avoid separating the buttonhole opening.

Hooks and Eyes

Hooks and eyes are hidden closures used in areas of the garment where there is little strain. They are also used to help button closures stay together at necklines and other areas that need additional control.

General-purpose hooks and eyes come in a range of sizes and two finishes—black and nickel. Each hook comes with two eyes—a straight eye and a round eye. Use straight eyes for edges that overlap and round eyes for edges that just meet.

Attaching Hooks and Eyes

Always sew the hook first. Set it ⅛ in. back from the inside edge of the blouse and use a whipstitch around each metal circle. Also secure the outermost end of the hook to keep it flat to the edge.

On a lapped edge, line up the edges to the closed position and mark where the end of the hook meets the underlap. Position the straight eye over the mark and whipstitch.

On a nonlapped edge, position the edges to the closed position and mark placement for the curved eye. Place the eye at the mark but on the underside of the edge so that it extends slightly past the edge. Whipstitch to hold in place.

COVERED SNAPS

Snaps come in a range of sizes and three finishes—black, nickel, and clear plastic. Covered snaps are a nice touch that you find on expensive silk blouses. You can purchase large covered snaps in basic colors, but if you want small ones, you'll have to cover your own. It is very easy to cover snaps as long as your fabric is lightweight and silky.

To cover a snap, cut a circle of lightweight fabric or lining large enough to enclose the snap. Place each snap section right side down on the wrong side of the fabric. Gather the ends of the fabric and enclose the snap. Use a hand sewing needle and thread to hold the fabric tightly around the snap. Wrap the thread around the fabric to hold the gathers tightly. Sew into the gathers to hold in place and cut away all excess fabric next to the stitches.

Sew the ball section of the snap to the back side of the overlap using a whipstitch. Overlap the edges to mark placement for the socket section. Rub tailor's chalk over the ball section, and when you line up the edges push down on the snap so that the mark rubs off on the other side. On light colors, you can use a lead pencil to mark the location of the socket section.

Easy Projects

Now that you know the tricks of the trade, try your blouse-making skills with this sleeveless blouse and reversible vest.

Sleeveless Blouse

This blouse is one of my favorites. Use this easy method to sew facings to sleeveless blouses entirely by machine. You can also use the same method to sew a lined or reversible sleeveless blouse or tank.

Sew the front to the back at the shoulder seams. Repeat for the facing (or lining). Press the seams open.

Pin the blouse to the facing at the neckline and sew (1). Trim and clip the neck seam. Understitch the seam allowances to the facing layer. (Don't understitch for a reversible garment.) Turn the garment right side out and press.

Pin all four armhole ends to the corresponding armhole ends of the facing or lining. Trim the facing or lining layer to be 1/8 in. smaller above the notches only (2). The lining does not need trimming near the underarm area.

To make an enclosed seam at the armholes, do the following for each armhole:

Roll the blouse from one side toward the armhole you will be sewing. Stop rolling when the rolled blouse is centered along the shoulder seam and next to the armhole (**3**).

Pin the armhole of the blouse and facing (or lining) with right sides together and the rolled blouse in between (**4**). Sew the armhole seam (**5**). Trim and clip the seam allowance.

Turn the blouse right side out and press the armhole seams. Reach into the shoulder and begin pulling the blouse to the right side (**6**).

1 *Sew around the neckline, and then topstitch or edgestitch if necessary.*

2 *Trim ⅛ in. from the edges of the armhole facing so that the fabric will roll to the inside.*

3 *Roll the blouse from one side to the other.*

Sew the side seams by matching underarm seams with right sides together. Sew the garment front to the garment back and sew the facing or lining front to the facing or lining back for each side. This should be one continuous seam. Clean-finish the side seams and the facing edge.

Sew the side seams together near the armscye to prevent them from rolling out. From the wrong side, fold the facing or lining to the front of the blouse along the armscye. Sew the side seams together (four layers), starting near the armscye for about 2 in. (7). Sew the hems separately.

4 *Pin the armholes, right sides together, with the rolled blouse inside.*

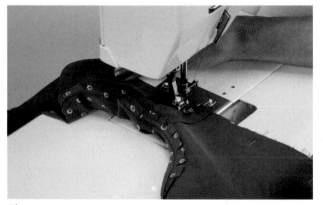

5 *Sew the armhole seam.*

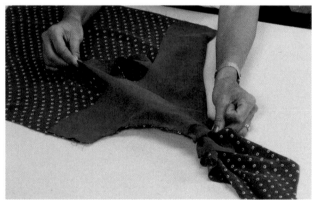

6 *Reach into the shoulder and pull the blouse right side out.*

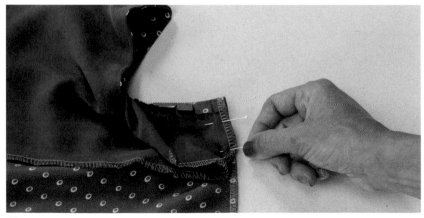

7 *Pin and sew the side seams together near the armscye.*

Reversible or Lined Vest

Here's an easy way to sew a reversible or lined vest. For best results, use the same fabric for both layers, such as cotton broadcloth or lightweight linen. Otherwise, be sure to select fabrics with a similar hand, such as cotton piqué and cotton broadcloth.

For a reversible vest, cut the lining fabric exactly the same as the outside fabric. For a lined vest, trim away 1/8 in. from the armhole seams and the outer edges of the lining layer. Do not trim the side seams.

If the vest has side front seams or front darts, sew these first. If the vest has a center back seam, side back seams, or back darts, sew them now. Do the same for the lining.

Press the seams open; no edge finish is needed. Sew the front to the back at the shoulder seams with right sides together. Sew the front lining to the back lining at

1 *Turn the vest right side out by pulling each front through the shoulder section.*

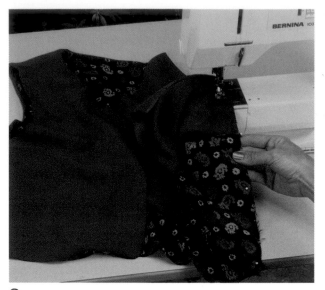

2 *Sew the side seams.*

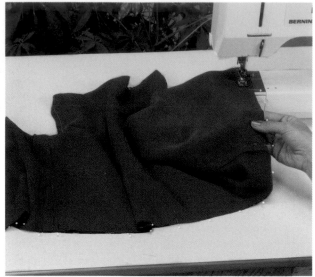

3 *Turn the vest wrong side out and stitch the lower edge, leaving a 4-in. opening.*

the shoulder seams with right sides together. Press the seams open.

Match the vest to the lining with right sides together at the front edge, back neck, and armholes. Stitch, trim, and clip the seams.

With the wrong side of the lining layer facing up, press the stitched seams open. To do this, press the lining seam allowance back over the lining and the vest seam allowance straight out.

Turn the vest right side out by pulling each front through the shoulder and back section **(1,** p. 109). Adjust and press the seams along the edge.

Sew the side seams **(2).** First pin the underarm seams so they are right sides together, and then pin the front to the back and the

front lining to the back lining. Sew one continuous seam. Repeat for the other side and press the seams open.

Turn the vest wrong side out through the bottom opening. Pin and stitch the lower edge, leaving a 4-in. opening **(3).** The best place to leave the opening is at the side back just beyond the side seam. Trim the seam to $\frac{3}{8}$ in. Trim any corners and clip any curves.

Pull the vest to the right side through the opening. Press the bottom edge. Edgestitch just the opening or the entire edge.

For a reversible vest, make buttonholes on both front edges and sew buttons onto a separate grosgrain placket.

Index

N

Neckline:
  finishes for, 64-67
  See also Collars.
Needles, choosing, 22
Notches, cutting, 39
Notions, discussed, 11-12, 14,
  21-23

P

Patterns:
  adjusting, 24, 27, 29-37
  choosing, 6, 11-13
  enhancing, 34-37
  envelope of, reading, 11-12
  and fabric selection, 12, 13
  multisized, 13, 31
  pin-fitting, 28
  simplifying, 24, 34
Pin-fitting. *See* Patterns.
Pinning:
  discussed, 46
  for silky fabrics, 50
Piping:
  cutting bias strips for, 40
  using, 65
Plackets, front:
  decorative, sewing, 102
  hidden, sewing, 101-102
  modifying, 36-37
Plackets, sleeve:
  continuous-lap, 87-89
  for "no-cuff" cuff, 94-95
  simplified, 90-91
Pleats:
  eliminating, 35
  marking, 42, 43
  sewing, 62
Pockets:
  adjusting pattern for, 37
  patch, sewing, 56-57
  welt, sewing, 58-60
Point turner, for collars, 55, 69
Press cloth, for fusing interfacing,
  55
Pressing:
  general guidelines for, 54
  tools for, 54, 55

R

Ribbing, knit, as edge finish, 66-67

S

Seam allowances:
  adjusting, 29, 31
  clipping, 53
  grading, 53
  notching, 53
  trimming, 53
Seams:
  bound, bias-tricot, 86
  double-stitched, 51
  eliminating, 35
  pinning, 46
  self-enclosed, 51-52
    bound, 52
    flat-felled, 52
    French, 51-52
  standard, 51
  See also Seam allowances.
    Sewing, directional.
Sewing:
  directional, defined, 48
  general guidelines for, 46, 47
  for silky fabrics, 50
Shoulder pads:
  attaching, 79
  discussed, 14, 22-23
  raglan, 22, 23
  removable, 79
  set-in, 23
Shoulders:
  seam of, repositioning, 32-33
  slope of, adjusting, 33
  width of,
    adjusting, 33
    measuring, 26
Silhouettes. *See* Figure types.
Silkies. *See* Fabrics, silky.
Size:
  chart of, 27
  and pattern adjustment, 27-28
  and pattern selection, 6, 12-13
Sleeve caps, sewing, 83-86
Sleeves:
  cutting on the bias, 34, 35
  dolman, 83
  dropped-shoulder, 29
  extended-shoulder, 29
  kimono, 29, 83
  length of,
    adjusting, 27, 29-30
    measuring, 26
  "no-cuff," 34, 36

raglan, 29, 83
set-in, 29, 83
sewing,
  flat, 83-84
  in-the-round, 84-86
shoulder pads with, 23
See also Cuffs. Plackets.
Slits, side, sewing, 100
Snaps, covered, discussed, 105
Stitches:
  for silky fabrics, 50
  types of, 49-50

T

Thread:
  choosing, 21-22
  for silky fabrics, 21, 50
Turn-of-cloth, adjusting pattern
  for, 34, 35-36

U

Understitching, discussed, 50

V

Vests, reversible, sewing, 109-110

W

Waist, measuring, 26
Width:
  adjusting pattern for, 30-32
  and ease, 30

Y

Yokes:
  back, eliminating, 34, 35
  blouse-type, 80-82
  cutting, 76
  facing for, 76
  sewing, 76
  shirt-type, 77-78